# Messages from the Dental Masters

## Mastering the Secrets of Successful Dental Practice

**Compiled by Dr Stephen Hudson**
**BDS, MFGDP, DRDP**

**SNH Publications LTD ©**

# Messages from Dental Masters

First publication in Great Britain
By SNH Publications Ltd

Copyright © SNH Publications LTD 2011

Visit the author's website at www.gdpresources.com

For information contact SNH Publications LTD, 2, Crown Close, Chesterfield, S43 2AH, UK
Distributed by SNH Publications LTD

# Contents

- Bruce Mayhew        **-87**
- Paul Mendlesohn     **-91**
- Barry Oulton        **-96**
- Ellis Paul          **-99**
- Raj Rattan          **-104**
- Alun Rees           **-112**
- John Renshaw        **-120**
- Steve Van Russelt   **-125**
- Sheila Scott        **-132**
- Joe Sullivan        **-137**
- Paul Tipton         **-143**
- Monik Vasant        **-148**
- Ian Wilson          **-157**

## Disclaimer

**For legal reasons, I am obliged to state the following**

Disclaimer: To the fullest extent permitted by law, SNH Publications Ltd are providing this written material, its subsidiary elements and its contents on an "as is" basis and make no (and expressly disclaim all) representations or warranties of any kind with respect to this material or its contents including, without limitation, advice and recommendations, warranties or merchantability and fitness for a particular purpose. The contributing authors are not psychologists or Independent Financial Advisors – **the information is given for entertainment purposes only**. In addition, SNH Publications Ltd does not represent or warrant that the information accessible via this material is accurate, complete or current. To the fullest extent permitted by law, neither SNH Publications Ltd nor any of its affiliates, partners, co-authors, directors, employees or other representatives will be liable for damages arising out of or in connection with the use of this material. This is a comprehensive limitation of liability that applies to all damages of any kind, including (without limitation) compensatory, direct, indirect or consequential damages, loss of data, income or profit, loss or damage to property and claims of third parties. The views expressed by the co authors are their own and are not necessarily endorsed by SNH Publications Ltd.

# Foreword

**"Only the wisest and stupidest of men never change"** - Confucius

Changes that affect society directly influence the demand for dentistry. During my time at the BDA, as a leading UK organisation for dentists, we examined such trends to understand and explain their impact on the profession. I will share some of my personal interpretations derived from this work.

- **Consider the following impending changes:**

- **An ageing population**

- **Mass immigration from Eastern Europe**

- **A recent fundamental reform to National Health Service Dentistry in 2006 and another expected 2013.**

- **Generation Y, who trusts dentists but don't know why and are the most consumer orientated youngsters ever.**

- **The Baby Boomer's generation, around 50-60 years old, who have had masses of restorative dentistry to keep their teeth functional**

- **A public seeking aesthetic benefits**

In my 10 year tenure on the British Dental Association Board of Directors I learnt to analyse our profession in macro terms, as it became my responsibility to see the national business of dentistry as a market. This article reflects on changes in the dental market, both as trends and possible future shape of the services.

When I first joined the BDA Executive Board, in 2000, dentistry was valued at ~£2 billion pounds. Boots had entered the market and their Marketing Director told me their forecasts were for the market to be worth £12-15 billion. In June that year the Financial Times had an A3 spread on comparing the UK to US dental markets. The FT noted that the US per capita spend was twelve times more than in the UK, potentially valuing the UK Market at over £24billion.

The current value of the UK dental market is believed to be ~£7.5billion. The forecast for 2015 was £15billion. With the current recession, that target date has been moved to 2018.

## Financial Trends in the UK dental market

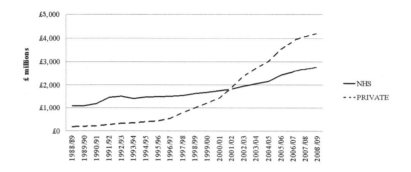

The graph vividly illustrates the major shift away from the NHS (state) service that dominated the provision of dentistry from 1948 onwards, to the private sector where dentists care for their patients against the other demands for their disposable income. That bodes well for dentists who understand that their successful future is based on pleasing their patients directly and not via satisfying some 3rd party's requirements. On the other side of the coin, it heralds the challenges that the profession faces too. For example, is Private work simply a case of

1. **Charging more than an NHS priced filling?**
2. **Placing composites instead of amalgams?**
3. **Doing more veneers than ever?**

What we think of the above will impact on our performance. The reality is that we need to understand why this is happening and what will motivate the patient to demand other services from us. After understanding we must use that information to guide us. Hence the rationale for creating this book. The principal author, Stephen

Hudson, has sourced some of the most informed minds to help us understand and then implement that knowledge.

My analysis for the rapid growth of Private dentistry is that NHS Dentistry is simply not a priority for Govt's of any colour. Against that our society is accessing more information and it empowers individuals to buy dentistry as a service that suits them. In short dentistry is becoming a lifestyle choice to purchases. If I had to explain that by grouping the services being purchased I'd place them into 3 components, using terms that patients use:

1. **Health**
2. **Beauty**
3. **Remedial**

Dentists see themselves providing the same services but using more familiar terms:

1. **Prevention –using more diagnostic devices to help the patient understand**
2. **Cosmetic treatments – both intra and extra oral**
3. **Restorative dentistry- from the traditional to the state of the art therapy of replacing lost teeth with new ones grown from stem cells.**

The relevance of this is twofold.

1. **Dentists have to understand that the patient is now becoming a consumer meaning that they will be less subservient in the relationship with dentists**
2. **Some distinct dental niches will begin to emerge.**

Examples of this abound when one opens any copy of the Yellow Pages or surf the web. The plethora of adverts show how some dentists have re-branded their practices to encourage specific groups of patients.
It's common to see

- **Dental spas**
- **Whitening clinics**

- **Specialist services such as Implant clinics and Adult orthodontics**
- **At least one company exists solely to provide children with sports mouthguards.**

Regarding the role of the Govt in our profession, I believe that the Govt will continue to support NHS dentistry, but not as we've known it. The above graph clearly illustrates:

1. **Neither Conservative or Labour Govt's prioritised dentistry by investing in it any more than necessary**
2. **Labour Govt has been disinclined to include dentistry within the massive increases it placed within the rest of the NHS.**

I believe that state commissioning will focus on the Govt to allocating money for the 20% of their population with the 80% of the disease. It's noted that most practices are not conveniently located there. What the Govt. wants is innovation to deal with that challenging issue and simply plonking a practice in an area lacking it does not guarantee a higher take up of dentistry amongst a population lacking that habit. But by using state of the art mobile practices, with up to 4 surgeries, to assess the demand before significant money is invested in setting up and maintaining new practices would be one example of innovation.

Clearly, this signals that dentists won't be conducting business as usual!

So the way forward is for dentists to decide if their future lies with sub-contracting to the NHS. Success, for those who remain in NHS service, is to comply with onerous regulations and look to innovate.

For those wishing to be involved in providing NHS dentistry, they need to know:

1. they will personally invest in the infrastructure that creates a practice
2. they have to retain or bid for new contracts
3. the new contracts pay on results, i.e. getting patients in through the door and providing treatment in accordance to NHS regulations
4. the new contracts intend to retain 10% of contract value and pay back on 100% compliance with new protocols called Dental Quality and Outcomes Framework (DQOF).
5. DQOF measures against
   a. Stabilisation or improvement of Oral Health
   b. Patient experience / customer service
   c. Patient safety
   d. Compliance with rules regarding oral health assessment, recall intervals and pathways of clinical care

So if we accept that change is inevitable, it is going to affect:

- **Funding - where we earn our money**
- **What we provide in delivering dental care that the State or patients want**

For those who simply want to care for their patients, without the aid or interference of a third party, the priority is to give their patients what they want. Give it to the best of their ability, seek appropriate training to upgrade skills and charge sensibly for it. They could always learn from an old sage about the value of the customer / patient

*"The patient is the most important visitor on our premises. He is not dependent on us. We are dependent on him. He is not an interruption of our work. He is the purpose of it. He is not an outsider in our business, he is part of it. We are not doing him a favour by serving him. He is doing is a favour by giving us an opportunity to do so."* - Mahatma Gandhi

If you prefer brevity:

*"Profit in business comes from repeat customers, customers that boast about your product or service, and that bring friends with them."* - W Edwards Deming

**Amarjit Gill BDS, MFGDP,** is a former BDA National President (2010-11) and current Chief Dental Officer for Practice Plan ltd, Chief Dental Adviser to Philips Healthcare and a practising dentist in Nottingham.

# Acknowledgements

I would like to thank all the co-authors who agreed to be involved in this publication. They take no financial reward for their part in this book and I am humbled by their participation.

I would also like to give a special thank you to Stuart Goldsmith who gave me the inspiration and the kick up the arse that was needed to get this book together.

Ladies and Gentlemen, let us begin.

# Preface

**"May you live in interesting times"** – Chinese Proverb

Sometimes Life comes along and gives you a slap about the head, just to make sure you are paying attention. It is in those brief times of crisis, when the world seems to be falling down around your ears, that the true nature of your character shines through. It is in these moments of decision that your destiny is forged.

I can remember the exact moment the idea for this book popped into my head. There I was minding my own business when this thought appeared out of nowhere.

**"You should publish a book. You should publish a book people will want to read"**

And here it is, in your hands, the results of almost a year's work. It was definitely worth it. When I approached the individual authors in this book for contributions, I had no idea what to expect from them. And I have to admit to being totally humbled by what they have produced. There is truth in this book. There is passion. And there is an honesty that is sadly lacking in today's society. I feel blessed to be associated with the people who have shared their knowledge and bared their souls to help you, the reader.

As dentists, we are living in one of the most exciting times in human history. We are here in a period of amazing technological breakthroughs, topped with a growing focus on the need for customer service and a patient focused experience. We no longer need to live in a world of Drill, Fill and Bill, although many of us still do. We are now moving into a world of prevention and minimal intervention dentistry, with the science of dentistry changing almost daily. The public's desire for cosmetic treatments increases every year and the dental health of a proportion of the nation seems to be on a spiral of endless improvement. There are now more opportunities for dentists than there have ever been, more skills to learn and more ways to show our excellence. We can if we so desire create a dental practice that would have been unimaginable even twenty years ago. We have the chance to spread our wings and fly.

But there is a rumbling darkness growing all around us. Our status as professionals is being ever eroded as statute law and litigation bite at our heels. Our once respected self regulation is slowly being stripped from us, whilst third party regulators impose the will of a confused government through threats of financial penalties and criminal sanction. There are now more obstacles and hurdles before us than there have ever been, and the provision of dentistry is becoming increasingly expensive and increasingly specialised. And all the time the bureaucrats and the lawyers circle like sharks waiting for their opportunity to display their self proclaimed importance. These are indeed interesting times.

And there you are right in the middle of it all just trying to live your life. And I'm sure that many of you will have noticed that dentistry can be a somewhat stressful job at times. There you are running 30 minutes late, the crown you have in your hand just won't fit no matter what you try, and you have just been told by your receptionist that Mrs. Jones is coming down with toothache from the root filling you did last week. There's a letter from a solicitor sat in your in box, you have 15 referral letters to do and you are behind with the staff appraisals. Of course there is one less appraisal to do because a staff member has just given you 2 weeks notice and another one has informed you that she is pregnant. Add an imminent CQC inspection, the recent palpitations you've been experiencing and the fact that your washer disinfector has just broken down, again, season with an angry patient sat in the waiting room and stir. Serve with a nice acid reflux vinaigrette.

Not a typical day, I'm sure you will agree... for most of us at least. But even when things are running smoothly, dentistry can be stressful. And it has always been like this, it's just that the nature of the stress is constantly changing. Twenty years ago, the big problem for most dentists was the new NHS contract and the fee cut (ending what had been, for some, a golden era). Here we saw the dawning of the NHS treadmill. Then there was the Dental Practice Board and their dreaded computer. Dentists were, on average, working too many hours, seeing too many patients and taking very little time off for themselves or their families, all in an attempt to make a living and keep their businesses viable. The result was a high burn out rate, a high alcohol/drug dependence rate and a surprisingly high suicide rate, as well as a gradual drift of dentists over to the private sector. I'll not talk about how many dentists had proved that the treadmill was an unnecessary burden, even in NHS practice. I'll not talk about how dentists, even working under the NHS terms of service, could make more money by seeing fewer patients. I'll not talk about how people like Chris Barrow were telling us 15 years ago to get rid of the heart sink patients and work smarter, not harder. No I'll not mention any of that. And I shall refrain from mentioning how the treadmill was not a creation of the system, but how the dentist worked within the system. My lips on that topic are sealed.

Things change of course, and in this present moment we have UDA's, clawback, HTM 0105, the CQC and a bubbling recession that has seen some private practices turnover drop through the floor. The question is still the same; it's just that the answers have changed.

### Q: "Why are dentists stressed?"

There are new global external stresses that potentially wait for all of us round the corner. But have you noticed a funny thing? Doesn't it seem that some dentists experience more stress and illness than others? I know some dentists who thoroughly hate their jobs, whilst others can't wait to get out of bed in the morning. I know some dentists who hit the wine bottle as soon as they are through their front door. Others hit the gym. I know some dentists who seem to be constantly handing money back to the PCT, whilst others succeed like never before, in private practice, in a recession that's apparently the worst since the invention of the air driven hand-piece. Some practices, it seems, have never been so busy.

So what's the difference? Why does one dentist struggle whilst a different dentist down the road seems to have the dream practice, with dream patients and a dream income? Both dentists may well have gone to the same dental school, were taught by the same tutors, and qualified in the same year together. They work in the same area, under the same system, but one struggles whilst the other prospers.

The way I look at it, it all comes down to the team leader. S/he creates the vision, creates the staff culture and sets the boundaries for what is acceptable. The difference between a struggling practice and a successful practice is down to two things: the space between the dentist's ears, and the dental practices ability to follow "**The Rules**".

So let's talk about "**The Rules**". In my opinion, there are preventable problems that dentists face, and these can be put down to several key factors. Surprisingly for some this doesn't include the CQC, or lawyers, or the GDC. Yes, they are an issue, but they aren't THE issue. For most of us they won't be career threatening problems. No, to me, the biggest threat in dentistry has always been Stress, and stress comes down to ignoring the key factors:

- **Seeing too many patients**
- **Working too many hours**
- **Seeing patients that we don't like and who don't like us**
- **Spending too much money/poor finances**
- **Making a living instead of taking time out to design a life.**
- **Doing dentistry that we don't enjoy**
- **Not knowing how to manage stress in the first place**
- **Running a practice that is not based on systems or ethical principles**
- **Ignoring the fact that your existing patient base is your number one marketing tool.**

Most dentists spend too much time doing dentistry. If you ask dentists who have cut back their working week to say four days from five, you hear time and again the mantra that by working fewer hours you make more money.  Not only do they make more money, but they also have a more pleasant practicing career.  I can guarantee, you will never hear a dentist on their death bed say "If only I had done just one more crown prep".

You see, as I am sure you are aware, dentistry is a very demanding job.  It is tiring to gaze into that tooth (or toothless) cavity eight hours a day.  Even the most committed dentist will need time to recharge, to refresh and to relearn.  Unfortunately many of us get into a pattern of slowly killing ourselves by working too hard whilst dancing on the edges of financial ruin.  Ask most IFA's and accountants.  They will tell you that dentists are AWFUL when it comes to handling money.  They are high earners, but they are also big spenders, and they seem to have an amazing habit of never saving up enough for the tax man.  And let's not even talk about their lack of business skills.

How would it be if you could spend your time doing a job you love, for people you like, making an income you are happy with, and still spend time with your family?  All that combined with the end result of becoming financially independent and living free from the shackles of being a wage slave.  Isn't that why you entered dental school?  Isn't that what you dreamed about when you were younger?  You see it is my philosophy that dentists should make it a life goal to become financially independent by the age of 55, and be able to survive in the world without their primary income.  Yes you heard it here first, by following the rules; I would argue that MOST dental practice owners can achieve millionaire status by the time they retire.

And is that the life you are living now?  Or are you too busy fighting fires to notice that you aren't living your dream.  So I have 10 questions for you to show you why this book was written:

- **Are you happy?**
- **Do you like your patients?**
- **Do your patients like you?**
- **Are you doing the dentistry you want to do?**

- Are you making the money you want to make?

- Does your job inspire you?

- Are your clinical skills where they should be?

- Do you enjoy the job you do?

- If you are a principal, are the business finances in good order?

- Are you living the life you want?

If the answer to any of those questions is no, then this book is for you. And even if you answered yes, the insights in the book humbled me, and I believe can help even the most successful practice.

Well, that's almost it from me folks. But before I pass you over to the real experts, I'm going to leave you with two quotes:

**"Be the change you want to see in the world"** – Ghandi

**"Everyone thinks of changing the world, but nobody thinks of changing himself"** – Tolstoy

You only have one life, so why not live it?

## Stephen Hudson BDS, MFGDP, DRDP
## www.gdpresources.com

# Chris Barrow

What they didn't tell you before you qualified as a dentist is that it's going to be tough, very tough.  Then again, they should have told you that at birth.

A profession that has the highest rate of alcoholism in the world and the second highest suicide rate after vets.  We may as well start off at the bottom and work upwards.

I want to address my comments to the 20% of you who are lunatic enough to want to set up your own business:

- **You cannot abide by somebody else's rules.**
- **You want to be free to make your own decisions.**
- **You are hard-wired for entrepreneurship - there's no arguing with the urge.**

In addition to all the clinical courses you are obliged and/or attracted towards, you will have to learn a brace of skills that they didn't teach you in the educational system or at dental school:

- **financial management**
- **marketing**
- **customer service**
- **compliance**
- **operational control**
- **employment and team-building**
- **leadership**

.....and when you have done with all that - add in a healthy dose of personal development.  You will have to:

- **become a good time manager**
- **work hard at being a good partner and parent**
- **keep yourself reasonably healthy**
- **exercise your brain and muscle outside of business**

In fact, all of that mind, body, spirit stuff - because any idiot can work 70 hours a week, take no holidays and become a very rich and very dull boy or girl.

I know because I've tried it (ah, the 90's).

It's running a business and staying happy and popular that takes effort and talent. So here we are, with yet another "self-improvement manual" to add to all the others. For goodness sake, hasn't it all been said by now?

- Decide on your core values. A set of guiding principles that will help you navigate through your journey.
- Have a strategy for the next 3 years (any longer than that and you will be overtaken by events and technology)
- Make a plan for the next 12 months and share it with your team and your family
- Establish personal and professional goals for every 90-day period
- Keep prioritised daily task lists. A, B, C the list and do the A's first
- Build a superbly well qualified and handsomely paid team around you.
- An internal team of employees and sub-contractors.
- An external team of professional and technical advisors and experts.
- Maintain balance in your calendar. 8 to 12 weeks vacation per year, plenty of long weekends, lots of time off and away from your business.
- Always, always watch the cash flow. It's lousy cash flow that kills the 9 out of 10 businesses that fail in their first 5 years.
- Constantly research on the web and at conferences to identify future trends - innovate as if your life depends on it.
- Avoid perfection - its stifles invention and experimentation.

*Read my free e-book **"The Perfect Imperfectionist"** to discover how I manage to use imperfection as a development tool.*

Have one constant in your life - change. Change everything, change it all the time, never stop changing things around you - drive people mad with your changes. The best business coach ever?

**Charles Darwin** - a species evolves by a process of continuous adaptation.

So that's the lecturing over with.

Everything you will ever need to know about to run a successful business will either be in your local book store or on the web (and most of it free to download). You would think it simple - just read the darned material and put it into action. So how come we are not all millionaires and super-success stories?

Why is it that, having been immersed in the personal and professional development movement since 1980, having read books, attended courses and mixed with the greats, that I'm not writing this on the rear deck of my 55 foot catamaran in the British Virgin Islands and emailing the copy to Steve before I swim with dolphins?

You can buy hundreds of books about how to "do it" but it seems there are not so many (apart from authentic business biographies) that explain why we don't. Do me a favour - if somebody tries to sell you a product or service that promises to miraculously transform your life - fat to thin, weak to strong, slow to fast, introvert to extrovert, dumb to smart, lonely to sex-symbol, poor to rich...

AND, if that person holds themselves out as a great (if not **THE** great) example of their own philosophy - then run a mile - **you are being sold snake oil**.

They conveniently ignore an important factor in self-improvement.

**Shit happens**

If you are going to survive the vicissitudes of life you will need to answer some important questions.

- **How many different types of shit are there?**
- **Where does the shit come from?**
- **How can you recognise it?**
- **What to do about it?**

So as I imagine my catamaran from the 09:05 Tiverton Parkway to London Paddington, putting in another long day that started at 05:00 and will end at 23:30, I want to talk to you about the shit that gets in the way of us **ALL** getting out of the rat race.

**Me very much included**. I'll be 58 years old when this is first published and I'm working as hard, if not harder, than at any time in my 41-year working life. Still haven't **"made it"** - still not out of the rat race. I have a theory I want to share with you. Ready?

### The shit is self-inflicted

We bring it on ourselves. There is nobody else to blame.

Let me take you on a journey back through my career and talk about some of the shit I've lived through and how it happened.

In the 80's I screwed up a promising career in a financial services corporate - left a great job and came back begging to return after 6 months.

### Why?

Because I was too busy having an affair with my secretary to focus on my career and family - **Self-inflicted**.

As my late father said at the time "there is nothing logical about an erect penis" - he was a man of few words but many of them were memorable. In the early 90's I presided over a business that went bust and, as a result, was forced to declare my own bankruptcy, losing a career and a family home.

## Why?

Because when my accountant called me into his office in February 1992 to tell me that my business was overtrading, that I would run out of cash and I needed to downsize, I replied with "no I don't, I'll sell my way out of this" - and a year later collapsed under the burden of debt - **Self-inflicted**.

OK - if a Jumbo Jet lands on your roof - its shit and it wasn't self-inflicted - there are disasters that strike, notably ill-health, whether it's you or a loved one. But most people struggle through life not because of Acts of God - but because of the amazing tendency that we have to self-destruct either when the going gets tough - or, amazingly, when the going gets great?

# Chris Barrow

**www.coachbarrow.com**
Coach, speaker, and business adviser who has worked with hundreds of dentists. Visit his website to find out more of what he could do for you today.

# Kevin Burch - Stress Free Dentistry

It's 11am on Friday, 29th April 2011, and Kate Middleton is about to step out of a Rolls Royce and into Westminster Abbey and her new life. And I, Kevin Burch, Confidence Coach, am stressed.

But my stress has nothing to do with the impending nuptials of Wills and Kate. In fact, I'm not even watching it - I am about to see a new client. I'm stressed because I am working - again - on this bank holiday, and the rest of my work is massively behind schedule. I don't know whether you, dear reader, have ever felt stressed because of overwork, unfulfilled expectations and missed deadlines, but if you have, read on.

You see, 50% of my clients are children and come to me from all across the UK and Ireland. Thus a quick "after school" appointment is not possible and the school holidays are some of my busiest times. It's rewarding work, and also very intense. And as well as being booked solid for the previous three weeks of Easter holidays, I've committed myself to seeing clients for three out of four of the bank holidays we have in this 11-day period. I want a break.

In addition to all this I've previously set myself some challenging deadlines for a new project I am undertaking - creating videos and other resources to make what I do available online. And, with the unexpectedly heavy workload of emotionally-demanding, face-to-face work I've been doing during this period, I have not met those deadlines. I am miles behind, in fact.

So here I am, physically and emotionally drained from my workload, and feeling a huge pressure to get on with my project. And this is the source of my stress. I'm making good money but working too hard **and am in danger of losing my inspiration for what I do**. The solution, as I see it, is obvious - to get a move on and actually do the work. But when I tell myself this something unfortunate happens: I feel even more pressure to get the work done and get even more stressed. I'm trapped in a vicious circle.

And then it hits me. I remember what the source of ALL stress is: thinking things should be different to the way they are. Let's say that again: **the source of all stress is thinking things should be different to the way they are.**

So I ask myself, "What do I think should be different?" And the answers come back, "I should be better at handling this workload rather than needing rest. I should be up-to-date with my deadlines rather than a long way behind. I shouldn't be stressed." OK, that's what's going through my head. And what if I tell myself, "It's OK that I'm tired and need rest. It's OK that I have done what I have done, and haven't done what I haven't done. It's OK that I've been feeling stressed." What if I try on this way of looking at things? So I do. And, in that moment, the stress disappears. The internal conflict has gone. I am relaxed. I am peaceful. I am happy.

I have stopped thinking things should be different, and instead **accepted them as they are.** And as a result I immediately feel so much better. Plus it is now easier, not harder, to actually get going and do the things I want to do!

This, my friend, is the difference between **accepting** things being the way they are, and **resisting** things being the way they are. It's a bit like getting upset about the weather. If you're away on holiday and it starts raining then broadly speaking you have two choices: either you say, "It shouldn't be raining, this is bad," which will give you one experience, or you say, "It's raining, that's the way it is, let's make the most of it," which will give you another experience.

**The question is: which experience do you want to have?**

Acceptance is a core practice in Zen Buddhism and other schools of Eastern thought. In Zen it is said that the gap between accepting things the way they are and wishing them to be otherwise is "**the tenth of an inch difference between heaven and hell.**" I love this quote, because it sums up how close together acceptance and resistance are - it really is like flicking a switch - and how at the same time they are poles apart in terms of the experience they give you.

I can hear you asking, "But if I accept things as they are, then I'll never bother to change things that need changing. OK, I can't change the weather, so that bit makes sense, but what about the things that I CAN change?" Which is a great question.

Picture this scenario: you're eating with friends at a restaurant and you order fish. When the waiter arrives with the food you discover he has got your order wrong and brings you chicken. How do you react? Are you upset, annoyed, irritated? What thoughts go through your mind in this situation? The reality is that there is chicken in front of you. This is how things are. This is exactly the same as the fact that when it is raining, it is raining. Now you have two choices. On the one hand, you can accept this reality, or you can resist this reality. Resisting it will not change it. It is what it is. While on the other hand, you can take action to change things, or not. You can ask him to bring you the fish you ordered, or you could go ahead and eat the chicken.

Whether you accept or resist the way things are, and whether or not you take action to change the way things are, are two different, separate choices. **This is the key distinction.** And thus they can exist in any combination, as shown in the table with the likely emotional experience (and some possible behaviours in brackets):

|  | **Taking action: Asking for fish** | **Not taking action: Eating the chicken** |
|---|---|---|
| **Resistance, thinking things should be different** | Upset, angry (short with the waiter, "this has ruined my evening, I'm paying all this money for good service," etc.) | Upset, angry (but not expressing it, or grumbling that "Well I want to eat with my friends so I'll put up with it.") |

| Acceptance that things are the way they are | Peaceful, calm (letting the waiter know you ordered fish and asking him to bring you fish, enjoying the evening regardless). | Peaceful, calm (enjoying the chicken, maybe telling the waiter what's happened, or maybe not). |
| --- | --- | --- |

Notice that whether you are upset or peaceful - the quality of your inner experience - is not determined by whether you ask for fish or stick with the chicken. All that choice affects is whether you have fish or chicken for dinner! What determines the quality of your experience is whether or not you resist the reality - the fact that you have before you, in the first instance, chicken. (As an important aside, you may also notice that the quality of your results is likely to be different, as well as the quality of your emotional experience - we all know what can potentially happen when we are rude to people bringing us food!).

Now, in the West we are often spurred to action by our resistance, by thinking things should be different. It is often being upset, a feeling of injustice, a sense of righteousness which drives our actions. This is true both individually and in groups (including at the level of large groups, otherwise known as nations) and sometimes this is obvious, and sometimes it is much more subtle. And actions driven by upset will have a certain quality to them and will get certain results. But consider this question that I like to ask any client of mine who is a parent: "When you held your first baby in your arms for the very first time, were you strongly motivated to take action to protect this baby, to care for this baby, to give this baby every opportunity in life?" You can guess their answer. And then I ask, "And were you motivated by being upset, by frustration, by fear, by anger, by jealousy, by a sense of 'things should be different'? Or was something else motivating you, and if so, what was it?" And, every single time, the answer comes back, "Love."

Consider that love is the strongest motivator for any human being. And when you take action because you love someone or something, or because you want to have fish, or because of the benefits your project will bring, you will have a very different experience - and tend to get different outcomes - to when you take action from a sense of "something is wrong, this should be different." One of the things about being human is that we all tend to resist things sometimes. We all want things to be different and get ourselves upset that they aren't (this includes wanting ourselves to be different, by the way; it includes thinking there's something wrong with us, that we should be different). And this is part of the human condition. And it's crazy. Because the more you resist, the more you will be upset, stressed, frustrated, whatever you want to call it. While the more you accept, the more you will be peaceful, relaxed and happy.

So, if you haven't already, think of a person, object or circumstance which is causing you stress, frustration, upset, etc. Ask yourself and honestly answer, "What is it that I am resisting about this person or situation? What is it that I think should be different?" Then, once you have your answer, ask yourself, "What would it be like if I accepted this, embraced it even, as OK, and simply the way things are?" And see what happens. You may or may not then take action - that's a separate thing. And then repeat this at other times and for other aspects of your life

Again.
                    And again.
                                        And again.

## Kevin Burch

## www.skyhighconfidence.com

Kevin works with clients of all ages and backgrounds, from Directors of publicly-traded companies to shy children, from England footballers, cricketers and rugby players to victims of abuse and trauma. A former assistant to Paul McKenna, his specialty is using cutting-edge psychological strategies and distinctions to bring his clients the lasting results that they require.

# Richard Charon - How Inhalation Sedation might improve your working life

**Declaration-** I am not paid by any company to advocate Inhalation Sedation. I do have an interest as I run courses to teach the technique.

In 2011, dentists have a multitude of roles and each must decide where their interest and emphasis lay. As well as being team leaders and marketers, orchestrating an increasingly vast array of regulatory and standards-based requirements, the bottom line is that dentists are primarily clinicians with a duty of care to their patients, ensuring the delivery of a high standard of technical but also ethical and empathetic care.

It is a *sine qua non*, that dentistry is a stressful occupation. As much as many of us enjoy it and as calm and professional as most of us are whilst undertaking our daily work, invading a person's intimate parts, their mouths, with invasive and potentially painful interventions, inevitably induces an increase in stress to our own systems. These biological and emotional stresses, cause rushes of adrenaline and the stress hormones, cortisol and noradrenaline, increasing heart rate, blood pressure and blood sugar levels, whilst we remain outwardly calm and sedentary. This is a toxic combination.

Then there is worry and concern about whether we are performing clinically as we should. Have I removed all of the caries? How near the pulp am I? Are my crown margins as sharp as they should be? Is that impression good enough? Shall I retake it? What about the cost in time and materials? Should I do this, that, or the other? The list is almost endless and all these type of decisions are taken in seconds or less, constantly throughout the working day. Day in and day out.

Now add to that heady mix, the whole issue of dealing with our patient's dental anxieties and indeed phobias and our own stress levels can soar, with long-term detrimental affects on our own health and well-being and indeed how we view our own professional lives as clinicians.

The 2009 Dental Health Survey shows that 48% of respondents had moderate to severe dental anxiety. So just about half of our working day, potentially at least, could be spent dealing with people with a degree of dentally related anxiety or indeed phobia. On top of that there is a medico-legal imperative to properly manage our patient's anxieties, with a potential for legal consequences should we fail to do so.

In my own 35 years as a dental clinician, the one single treatment modality that has had the greatest benefit, not just to the oral health but also to the lives of my anxious patients and therefore to me, is the use of Inhalation Sedation or "Relative Analgesia" (RA). I have used RA on a daily basis, about once per day on average, so something in excess of 7000 administrations, for adults and children since 1977.

Apart from its obvious uses of helping anxious patients to accept routine dentistry, more than that, it enables more ambitious treatment plans, (within one's own competency) to be delivered to patients who otherwise would be unable to tolerate this level of treatment complexity.

Orthodontic impressions for adults, who had previously had to abandon treatment as youngsters, as they their gag reflexes prevented impression taking.

Adults who had put off periodontal, endodontic, restorative dentistry (perhaps all three for the same patient) needed to salvage a failing dentition, resulting from their unwillingness to seek treatment through their anxiety.

In terms of improving your working life, how would it be, if carrying out your operative dentistry, with an anxious patient, were to be like working on a phantom-head again? Remember those days? Prepping cavities and crowns with no tongues, no wriggling, no tears, no fidgeting, no upset, no constant reaching for another mouth rinse and NO STRESS for you?

Well working on a patient, child or adult, sedated with RA, is just like that. What's more their recovery is very rapid too. *Ipso facto*, LESS STRESS for you!

I fully accept that this technique will not suit all anxious patients but my own experience is that I can manage 95% of dental anxiety cases with this method. For the others I do use Intra-venous Midazolam or refer to a hypnotherapist those who have a psychologically based true phobia. This is not the place to explore this in further detail though.

Here are just a very few quotes from people who have been able to receive their dental treatment using RA, that they would otherwise have put off and so suffered pain, infections, misery and social embarrassment.

> *"Thank you so much, you have fixed a broken part of my personality"*

Here is the relief felt by one patient via a Tweet in July 2011. She had attended a couple of days previously with an upper 3rd molar erupting buccally and causing mucosal ulceration.
The tooth was extracted with RA and LA. She wrote *"Astounding treatment today from @RichardCharon. I will never fear tooth removal again! Having Tweeted this, she has then sent a longer testimonial. Here it is...*

*"Having had a stubborn wisdom tooth removed a few years ago, I wasn't particularly looking forward to having another one extracted. Until I met Richard & Chris at Newbury Smilemakers! They put me completely at ease about the treatment and, with the help of Richard's 'Happy Air', the treatment went amazingly quickly and smoothly. In fact, I couldn't believe it when Richard said it was over - I'd only been there a few minutes! Post-op has been great too - no swelling and I've barely needed the painkillers!*

*I just wish I'd found Newbury Smilemakers earlier - I'll definitely be going back and recommending them."*

Now wouldn't this outcome be one to be proud of and improve your working life? What a fantastic service to be able to give this patient, with the prospect of receiving word of mouth referrals from her too and perhaps some of her Twitter followers as well. So this is one simple example of how my clinical challenge was made much easier, the patient was delighted at the outcome and as a result there is additional potential to further build my practice.

And here is another patient's comment:

*".... I would like to see nitrous oxide used in every dental practice, as many people I know have at least some level of dental anxiety. As a businessman I would have thought that this represents a good revenue opportunity for most dental practices as well as a great marketing opportunity to attract more anxious patients. Overall, the combination of nitrous oxide and the professional and kind treatment of Richard and Chris has gone a long way to restoring my faith in the dental profession."* Matt.

... and one last one:

*"Just to say thanks again to you and Richard for having a go at fixing that tooth for me yesterday and for explaining about the veneers. Sounds like that is next course of action. Just a shame I didn't find you earlier, as I may have been able to save my teeth from being in the state they are now! I know you now have a complaints procedure but I'm not sure if you have a 'compliments' one. In case you do then thanks again for helping to restore my faith in dentists and making it much easier to visit the dentist! (the happy gas is also fabulous!)"* Zara

There are more like that at http://www.newburydentist.co.uk/59.html. So these are the sorts of responses we receive as a result of being able to offer RA as a service to our patients and using the technique as a tool in our armory, on a daily basis.

If you want to delve further, I have assembled more than twenty case histories to illustrate the success I have had over the years. Also a number of my patients have provided their own detailed stories, in their own words, of how they were helped, in different ways using RA as well as many additional testimonials
**http://www.the-ra-coach.co.uk/22.html**

Such is the profoundly beneficial effect that this technique has had on my own working life, that I decided to help spread the word. In my opinion and that of others too, the scope and usefulness of the technique is poorly understood in the UK amongst GDPs. In 2001, as a result of some inspiration from Chris Barrow, I developed a one-day teaching course, which I have run four or five times a year, since 2003. They are usually delivered from my own private practice in small groups of 5-8 people, aimed at all members of the dental team. For larger groups to a maximum of 16 usually, alternative venues are used. By invitation, the course has, to date, been delivered three times in the Republic of Ireland and once in Northumberland with current plans to run it in the Manchester area in the autumn of 2011.

If I have convinced you of the benefits of this technique then why not consider introducing it yourself? Here are just three testimonials about the teaching day/courses that I run. There are very many more here. I hope they inspire you.

*"One of the best, if not the best, one day independent course we've had the pleasure of attending! I first used RA 25 years ago and discarded it in favour of IV. Now, 25 years later I'm returning to the fold and it was an honour to relearn it all from the Master himself -Richard Charon. The commitment is made, equipment is being ordered and we already have a queue of clients desperate for it. If anyone is considering RA, my advice is Contact Richard, book the course, do it, buy the kit and tell ALL your clients - they really, really want it, you just didn't know."*

*Cheers - Dave n' Barb*
*From Dave Naisby , GDP in Inverness 2010.*

Jenny Pinder, ex-GDC member and herself focusing on providing care for the dentally anxious and phobic.

*"One of my achievements this year has been to incorporate RA into my toolbox. Thanks to Richard and his course. It took a while to get round to it but I got the new <u>digital RA machine</u> from <u>RA medical</u>, and it's very easy to get the hang of. I've done 10 cases now, and feel more comfortable, a very supportive dental nurse, who also came on the course with me, has been a blessing .*

*Jenny, never too old to learn something new. 10th Dec 2006"*

*"Super Patient <u>AND</u> Practitioner centered course. Will affect + direct mu professional practice for years to come. Lecture notes are excellent.*
*Thanks Richard and Chris"*

Paul Cochrane, from Northern Ireland

I think by now you will have the idea. Me, only a BDS? I did once apply to undertake a Dip Sed. and was informed by a leading figure in the world of UK dental conscious sedation, that I was "too experienced and should be giving out certificates and not trying to gain them". So I was politely refused entry.

I have also been told and given permission to quote, from another senior member and trustee of SAAD, that given my *"exemplary record, I was in a better position than SAAD to provide competency certification for DCPs"*.

**Richard Charon BDS**

**www.the-ra-coach.com**
**email: richard@the-ra-coach.co.uk**

# Rob Dyas - 10 ways to improve your working life

When your passion is your work it is very easy to lose the distinction between work and the rest of your life. Work can overwhelm everything else. I love my business but I also value time spent with my family and friends.

My father died when I was quite young and I think almost certainly that is what has given me the drive. He worked all his life aiming for retirement and to keep his family, he never got there! I only ever remember one family holiday together. It has always been very important to me. We travel regularly and widely, even though my children are still in junior school.

I am the director of RD Online Dental Learning a rapidly growing blended dental learning website with articles, videos, and webinars. The company started in 2008 following on from my background in undergraduate and postgraduate education. I used to organise both regional and national courses for the whole dental team, and the question I always used to ask is why can't some of this be done online. Today we have over 11,000 subscribers, and over 150 hours of verifiable CPD are done on our site every day. Also around the world and via the World Health Organisation people in certain developing countries have completely free access. I believe passionately in giving back. We give significant proportions of our profits to Bridge2Aid a dental charity which trains clinical officers, and I am going back to Tanzania to work with them again in 2012.

One of the greatest gifts for me professionally was to learn the word "no." Always push the boundaries but if you know it is wrong don't do it! I have been really lucky in my professional career to have worked with some fantastic people, and one of the things I learnt was that I would need a mentor throughout my career. I think it is essential, so much so that I trained to be a mentor, which I still am to dentists, doctors and nurses.

Harness the motivating power of your other passions. No matter how passionate you are about your business don't pretend you are one-dimensional.

In the mornings I have certain aspirations. One of my goals is to avoid looking at my computer or checking my email for at least an hour after I wake up.

I like to read first thing in the morning. I'm addicted to the Kindle. I read a lot of business books, because I feel I should work out how to be a real businessman before someone works out I am not. I also love reading autobiographies, and I have always been fascinated by other people's stories. Reading is my buffer into the day.

We rarely have meetings. I hate them. They're a huge waste of time, and they are costly. It's not one hour; it's 5, because you pulled 5 people away from their real work. Also I hate it when businesses treat their employees like children. They block Facebook or YouTube because they want their employees to work eight hours a day. But instead of getting more productivity, you're getting frustration. What's the point? As long as the work gets done, I don't care what people do all day.

I am still a wet fingered dentist (oral surgeon) which I love, and most of my clinical time is involved with dental implants. Let me just say that again I am a dentist and I love my job! I have placed well over 10,000 implants in my career and am one of the main directors of the ADI (Association of Dental Implantology). Why take this on as well as my other commitments? Because I passionately believe I can make a difference, I have a clear vision for where I think the ADI needs to be.

In my home office, I have three Mac computers (have used Mac now for over ten years, I cannot understand why anyone would use a PC). I also have a laptop (MacBook Air), which I have with me all the time.

One of my favourite programs is Filemaker by Bento. It allows me to keep track of all my various projects, and ideas. I love coming up with new ideas. I have so many emails that come in (up to 250 per day) and one thing I realised was that I was checking my emails every few minutes, and thus never actually getting any work done. Now I check emails only 5 times per day. With so many potential demands on my time I have tied to automate as much as possible. For example we now have a new automated e-flyer system that will automatically collect data from our website and send it out to people based on dental specialty. This we completely developed from scratch, and now we are going to be selling the concept to others.

At the end of each day I write down 5 things I will accomplish the next day. This helps keep me focused. It's easy to waste time in the morning. You can get started straight away without losing that start up time.

I listen to music every day, all sorts of music, when I am working, wherever I am working, whilst traveling. Also I still play music as I did when I started university in Sheffield in the 1980's. I play both keyboards and guitar. I still gig regularly with my band the **Likely Ones** which we have had together for over 3 years. We rehearse every week and play 15-20 times per year. The lead singer of my band at university "Bomber and the Grahams" went on to become a famous comedian and actor (but that's another story).

Live where you want to live. I always had a dream from when I was a university student to build a house where we live. This we did nearly 8 years ago now, we even discussed being filmed for Grand Designs, but as they said to us, they would only show it if things went wrong. We decided against having our angst televised!

Set aside blocks of uninterrupted time to focus on what's really important to you. One of the biggest challenges I had in figuring out my own work-life balance was my children. They deserved my uninterrupted attention sometimes, and when I was juggling my full time job and my burgeoning website, it was very difficult. The way I managed it was to realise that time with my children every day was of paramount importance, and so I just scheduled a three hour block of time each day that I spent solely with my family. We ate together, played together, read stories together, and so on.

When I first met my wife I used to carry around an old note book with 25 things I wanted to do before I died. That list has been changed many times over the years, things done, things changed, things added. Yes, I still have 25.

Do I have long term plans for all of our various companies, yes, but for the time being I will keep those to myself!

Top Tips to help improve your working life:

1. Switch your phone off in the evening
2. Work through lunch, you will get home earlier
3. Only look at emails 5 times a day
4. Work hard
5. Play hard
6. Make a difference
7. Find a mentor
8. Spend as much time as you can with your parents (while you can)
9. Spend as much time as you can with your kids (while you can)
10. Get enough sleep

**Robert Dyas**
**BDS DCH MMedSci FDS RCS**
**Oral Surgeon**
**Director ADI**
**Director RD Online Dental Learning**
**www.rdsurgery.com**

# Philip Greene

> Whenever I feel afraid,
> I hold my head erect
> And whistle a happy tune, and no-one will suspect
> I'm afraid.

You get out of your car, pick up your bags, and walk to your practice door. You open the door. You walk in.
Your reception team is already in position.

"Good Morning," you say, "How are we today?"
"Fine," comes the reply. Or "Mr Greene, it's Monday MORNING!!!"
Or, worse, "Not too bad."
"Let's try that again."
You go out again.
You come in again.
**"Good Morning,"** you say. **"How are we today?"**
"BRILLIANT. FANTASTIC. NEVER BETTER," you hear, (because they're used to your funny little ways by now) and don't you all feel so much better when you start each day on a positive note?

Emotions follow your body language, you see, so if you stand up straight, put a smile on your face and say you feel great, then you WILL feel great. And each day, each conversation, starts on a better note than before.

Richard Rogers and Oscar Hammerstein understood this before anyone had heard of Richard Bandler and NLP (of which more later). They wrote *The King and I* in 1950.

> The result of this deception
> Is very strange to tell
> For when I fool the people I fear
> I fool myself as well.

It's your attitude that counts. First you have to love what you do. If you don't, you need to change something. It may be that you would be happier in another branch of dentistry, (as a researcher or in sales, or teaching, for instance) or that you should try to change your working environment. There are only three ways of dealing with circumstances that make you unhappy. Here they are:

**Accept it.**
**Change it.**
**Leave it.**

And that's it.
So you can improve your working life very easily.
But first, you need to know what you want.

When you set out on any journey you normally know where you are going. And most of the time you get there, even if you make a few detours on the way. So why do so many people embark on the journey of their lives without knowing where they want to get to? What do you want to achieve in your career? What would you like to have said about you when you retire? Or when you shuffle off? And what are you doing to bring it about?

Very few people actually sit down and think about these issues, so if haven't done it yet you are not alone, but help is available through books, seminars and life coaches, especially the dedicated dental ones. For the more independent, self-help books and courses are readily available.

The *Pankey Philosophy* is a good place to start. Originally presented by L.D. Pankey as The Cross of Dentistry, it goes like this,

- **Know yourself.**
- **Know your patient. (Never treat a stranger)**
- **Know your work.**
- **Apply your knowledge.**

They say that knowledge is power but they're wrong. The power is in the *use* of the knowledge. Action is the key because knowing and not doing is like not knowing. Try to get a candle to go out just by thinking about it. You can't, but a little action produces the result you want. **Action is the Key**!

Next you need a solid base of values on which to build your goals. *The Seven Habits of Highly Effective People* by Stephen Covey (www.stephencovey.com/7habits/7habits-habit1.php) provides a basis for living a useful and fulfilling life by understanding and prioritising what is important to you. You could also read the inspiring work of Viktor Frankl, *Man's Search for Meaning*. Then, progress to Anthony Robbins' (also excellent on CD or DVD) *Unleash the Power Within.* (www.tonyrobbins.com)

Then develop your life skills by reading *Getting to Yes* by Roger Fisher and William Ury and *Influence, Science and Practice* by Robert Cialdini and your business skills with *The E-Myth* by Michael Gerber. (www.e-myth.com) and *Building the Happiness Centred Business* by Paddi Lund. (www.paddilund.com)

After this basic grounding you are ready for Neuro-Linguistic Programming, better known as **NLP**, a toolkit for peak performance in every aspect of your life. The study of NLP will improve all aspects of your life by helping you to understand and build rapport with anyone you come into contact with, and show you how to be at your best whenever you want.

Of course, these life skills apply to your professional life too, and now that CPD is unavoidable there is now a profusion of training opportunities to choose from. You may even want to develop a special interest or specialise in one aspect of dentistry. Postgraduate training is available.

All this education will need modern updated working methods, of course, so you will need to work smarter; computerised information technology, digital imaging, lasers, CAD-CAM all have a place in modern dentistry.

You see it's not all about technical skill – that's important of course but it comes with practice and experience – but about how your knowledge and skill can help others. The satisfaction you get from a grateful patient is worth more than the fee!

Self-improvement is the overarching goal, trying to maximise your potential. If you can achieve this, you will improve not just your working life, but the entirety of your existence.

Now, what was it you wanted the rest of us to say about you?

**Philip R. Greene BDS, FDSRCPS, CUEW, JP.**

Specialist in Periodontics and postgraduate lecturer

**www.effectiveperio.co.uk**

**prgreene@sky.com**

# Martin Haines - How Regulation Has Changed the Financial Services Industry

Broadly speaking the financial services industry we have today was created in the 70s and 80s. The boom years meant that families had some spare cash to spend, the obsession with property as a single asset class was somewhere in the future and the failure of successive governments to control inflation meant that share values were increasing at a phenomenal rate year-on-year. All of a sudden more and more money was put into savings and investments rather than largely being left on deposit with building societies. Insurance companies, ever the creators and innovators, were quick to see the opportunity and financial "products" flooded into the market. New companies emerged like Abbey life and Allied Dunbar creating massive direct sales forces that were employed from virtually every other industry, eventually they became so short of recruits that quite frankly by the mid-80s if you could fog up a mirror an insurance company would employ you.

Although many consumers benefited from this process the ever-increasing rush for ever greater commissions created a melee of greed, mis-selling misinformation and a "devil take the hindmost mentality". Horror stories started to emerge and the government started to make louder and louder noises eventually threatening the industry with "**regulate yourselves or we will do it for you**". Needless to say no individual company was going to change unless all the others did and the only other possible motivation to change would be if they were compelled to by an external force. Finally the government of the day, exhausted by the continuing abuses, brought about the Financial Services Act 1986. Created by an Act of Parliament and passed by the government of Margaret Thatcher it brought in a mixture of governmental and self-regulation. There followed a raft of entities and regulators, culminating in the Financial Services and Markets Act 2000 which created the Financial Services Authority (FSA). The FSA has teeth, unlike in my opinion some of the other regulators governing other professions, and they know how to use them. The whole industry is now working towards RDR

(Retail Distribution Review) which comes into effect on 31 December 2012.

Among many directives there is a requirement for all those giving advice to be qualified to a suitable standard and not before time there is an attempt to break the stranglehold of commission on the advice process. IFA's will be compelled to offer their clients the option of paying by fees with commissions received being rebated either to reduce the cost of a given product or reinvested to enhance an investment or rebated to the client or used to offset the fee. A handful of companies including my own have been offering the above option to clients for many years and just occasionally it really pays off to be that far ahead of the game. Interestingly RDR has a very heavy emphasis on "ethics" which is borne out of the realisation that regulation and punishment can only go so far in forcing people and companies to change their behaviour. There are still far too many examples of the most highly qualified and high profile businesses giving poor advice, but the overall situation is vastly improved from the bad old days before 1986. The FSA have stated that what is really needed is for companies and individuals to "regain a sense of what is right and wrong", in other words to genuinely put the client's needs before their own. Sadly I can tell from the amount of remedial work that we are called upon to carry out that the above sentiment is still not at the heart of all financial adviser operations.

## So is there anything the dental profession can gain from the financial services experience?

The first lesson has to be don't fight it; more than 70% of the directives now existent in the financial services profession originated in Europe. The process is inexorable and any attempt to hold back the tide will be a complete waste of energy. Leave your professional associations to argue over the detail where they can and then just get on with it. Take what little consolation you can from the fact that it's happening to everybody and every business. The cost of increased regulation will and must fall on the end user so the need for a properly structured fee scale and regular fee increases has never been greater. If you don't have the resources in the practice then buy them in, get on with what you do best and that is earning a living through dentistry. It's not for me to comment on the quality or otherwise of dentistry being delivered in the UK, that's for dentists to consider, but from the conversations I have week in week out with dentists throughout the UK it is clear that many of you have grave concerns. CQC etc may seem to have some very strange and unrelated requirements, but many believe it will become a useful tool to remove the very worst of practitioners, the vast majority of course have very little to fear.

Take heart, those of us who have always believed in quality financial advice went through a period of stamping our feet and banging our fists, but now, grudgingly perhaps, we have embraced the principle of regulation. The vast majority of regulation is a sledgehammer to crack a walnut, but our regulators have genuinely developed a dialogue with the profession, they know that a healthy and vibrant financial services industry is absolutely vital to the UK consumer and to the economy. There can't be many professions more important than dentistry so hopefully your regulation will bring about higher standards where they are required.

## Which type of financial adviser should you choose?

Broadly speaking the majority of the financial advice available in the UK (excluding basic or non-technical advice) comes in four different forms.

**Tied advisor.** Tied advisers work with a limited range of products from one/a small panel of companies. They are only allowed to advise on the products available to them and if none of the products are suitable they must confirm to the individual they are unable to help. They cannot recommend a "next best fit". There is no requirement to compare those products with the open market. However, because markets and products are now so broad, it is impossible for anyone company to have a range of products large enough to suit every situation and need.

**Multi-tied advisor.** An individual who has an agreement with a number of different companies and can market a range of products from each of those companies, but the advice will still be restricted to a certain extent in that there is still no requirement to compare those products with those available in the open market.

**Whole of market advisor.** Must make a recommendation from the whole market and is required to find what would be deemed the most suitable product available from all companies as opposed to a tied advisor who is only required to look at one or a range of companies.

**Independent financial advisor (IFA)** like the whole of market advisor must also make a recommendation from the whole market but crucially must also offer their clients the opportunity to pay a flat fee for the advice.

So which one should you choose? For those who need to purchase financial products it is tempting to say who cares about the commission as long as I don't have to pay a fee, but as you might imagine somebody always pays the commission and yes it is you. That said if you have a very small amount of money to invest but still need advice a tied or multi-tied advisor might be the best choice.

## Why fee-based financial advice is so important

Commission in theory is a lump sum payment in return for the promise of ongoing service for the "lifetime" of a product or policy. It's hard not to let a cynical smile breakout on your face when you consider that concept. It never has worked that way nor will it ever which is why the regulators are finally getting to grips with it. There are other problems associated with commission namely poor cash flow, lumps of cash sometimes quite large come at various intervals meaning that most financial advisers suffer cash flow problems in a system of "feast and famine" which means they often neglect to invest money in their businesses, systems and staff. It's almost impossible not to be swayed by a large lump of cash available for giving advice on one policy in comparison with the few pounds that may be available with another. Regular fees provide far superior cash flow and if properly implemented completely remove the need to consider commissions at all. As a dentist you earn your living by charging fees so when you require quality technical financial advice, if you can afford to, always pay a fee for it. By all means shop around, every financial adviser has to state what their fees are before they start work and the cheapest won't always be the best but conversely why pay more than you need to.

## What type of advice could I receive?

Potentially you could receive advice on a whole range of financial issues and products but broadly speaking unless you have requested specific advice on one single issue and unless your financial advisor has stated that he or she is offering restricted advice you can expect to receive advice in the following areas:

**Protection** will include life cover, income protection, private medical insurance, critical illness cover and if you're advisor is dental specific you will receive advice on policies relating directly to the practice.

**Retirement** is a very broad subject that could include ISA's, investments and property, but typically focuses on all types of pension planning to include stakeholder, personal pension plans, self invested pension plans usually with a property element and all reviews should include a detailed analysis of any superannuation benefits relating to NHS income.

**Savings and investments** once again cover a broad area, but typically involves bank and building society deposits, National Savings, existing endowments and savings plans, shares, cash and shares ISA's, Friendly Societies plus the many pooled or collective investments and bonds

**Business planning and advice.** This is the main area where things have changed and are changing. I alluded to it in my title, but it is important to realise that many experienced independent financial advisers have become facilitators and arrangers who now have an oversight role concerning most or all of their clients business and financial needs. "Big picture" financial planners who are actively looking at a clients short, medium and long-term goals are uniquely placed to advise on when and where fellow professionals should be brought in for technical or additional advice. Strong and mutually supportive associations have been formed with companies such as accountants, lawyers, IT specialists, specialist business planners, HR consultants, practice development specialists, coaches and specialist marketing companies. Remember to make sure there is no financial connection between your financial advisor and these associated companies, if there is they may be reluctant to sever the relationship when they fail to deliver.

Dentists can and do spend enormous amounts of money on the wrong or incompetent advisers. A typical example I came across recently was where a marketing company had promised a practitioner that if he invested circa £10,000 new patients would be falling over themselves to get through the door. The money was duly spent, the patients didn't arrive and there was absolutely no means of redress. It is the job of the IFA if he is a specialist in a given profession to evaluate such businesses and to know beforehand whether or not they will deliver. Obviously this requires a very detailed and extensive knowledge of a given profession.

In my own case I started working with dentists in 1990 and after five years realised that if I was going to be able to really help dentists I would have to take time out to learn how the dental profession actually worked. In 1995 I temporarily stopped working as an IFA, handed all my non-dental clients to my business partner and went to work for Denplan as regional manager for one year. The next two years were spent with a specialist independent dentist only IFA in London. Then came another two years with a dentist only specialist accountant. After five years out I re-formed my own business, renamed it Dental Financial Associates, and created a fee-based remuneration structure and from then on accepted only dentists as new clients. Because we consistently refuse to work with any other profession outside of dentistry we are totally and completely focused on only the issues that affect dentists. This allows us to create a detailed financial plan to include all protection arrangements, savings and investments plus a stand-alone retirement plan that importantly doesn't rely on the sale of your home or the sale proceeds of the practice. To gain a total grasp of how we achieve that you might find it helpful to read two articles I published that are on my website entitled "Rolling Net Worth versus Conventional Financial Planning" and "Pensions To Invest or Not to Invest -That Is the Question". Within the plan we produce a total cost analysis, if the cash isn't available with our help the practitioner can fine tune the practice to provide the necessary funds. It's very like treatment planning, you take the x-rays, create a treatment plan and then you discuss payment methods with the patient. If cash is available and there is patient willingness to get on with it you get them booked in and complete all the work as required, alternatively you may well spread the work required over 18 months or two years which can make the treatment and the payment much easier for the patient. Working this way with your financial advisor can actually save enormous amounts of cash and as importantly create real peace of mind by making all your financial plans predictable. It may be interesting to note that many of our clients achieve all their financial goals within their existing budget and the vast majority of the rest need only increase their gross fee income by around 4%.

DFA is not unique, I wish it were, and so you don't need to take on just any financial adviser. Make sure you are dealing with a specialist, check out his or her website and very importantly check out the testimonials carefully, these will tell you how effective the businesses is and to what depth it is able to work.

**In summary** there is no doubt that the dental profession is going through trying times, but all the statistics show an increasing amount of money is being spent on dentistry year-on-year. With the right mindset and the right advisers the future will be happy and profitable.

**Martin Haines** is proprietor of **Dental Financial Associates** who are specialist independent financial advisers working exclusively with the dental profession.

**www.dentalfinancialassociates.co.uk**

# Keith Hayes

Being asked to write a chapter has made me stop and think, reflect, let go a little... So here goes. I used to suffer from paranoia, now I found out why: **they *are* out to get me**.

Ok an old joke, but it has meaning for me. At stressful times my old nervous tick will come back to haunt me, just when I think I have it all under control.
**Let me take you back 50 years**.

When I was eight, my mostly absent Dad left home for good. As an only child, I was instantly promoted to head boy of the household! Mum worked hard and long hours to provide for us and fortunately I pretty soon **'got it'** that I needed to be successful and earn a living. Fortunately at that time (1963) the education system IMHO was at its best. I, of course, went to State schools and realised that life in the future was most likely to be 10% inspiration and 90% perspiration and consequently I worked hard to pass exams. I succeeded (just) in passing the 11 plus and gained a place at grammar school.

My decision to study Dentistry was carefully crafted one lunchtime while playing cards in the Biology lab with my best friends – one of whom had a sister (I secretly much admired) who had just started at Guy's. So there we are, decision made. In the back of my mind was always a feeling of vulnerability. It was always something of an embarrassment to admit that my parents were divorced (in 1963 it was not so common) and also that my Mum worked as an office cleaner (so did I to help out) and that we were on the 'housing register' in case my Dad ever decided to throw us out, (he never did). From this point onwards I determined to make myself less and less vulnerable.

Dentistry is a difficult and stressful business and we all need a means of dealing with this. This is mine and I hope you might find it useful in parts.

Knowledge is power and I decided that I would acquire it as quickly as possible from the best source. My best friend's sister had chosen Guy's Hospital because they were getting a posh new building at London Bridge and she had put them first on the UCCA form (remember the politics). I had put Guy's first and they told me all about how they had the best building and I put The London Hospital, Whitechapel last because they didn't mind apparently. When I went to the London for interview, they showed me what they were doing in caries research and oral medicine and they wanted me to be a part even though I wasn't terrific at rugby, decision made.

That summer (1973) I started working as a hospital porter at the London Hospital with special responsibility for delivering the post to anyone who was anything in the Dental Institute. Nobody else wanted that job because the Institute was like a rabbit warren and before long I was promoted to opening and locking up the Institute, organising parking arrangements and by the start of term I knew just about everybody in the Dental Institute. Better still I had made many friends and was developing a real thirst for knowledge about Dentistry. There can be nothing better than working at a chosen pastime which will also become your living.

I have never been the best strategic planner in the world and being blessed with the memory of a goldfish means that I need to plan short hops on my path to success. To be honest back in 1973 I probably would have defined success in a totally different way to how I would think of it today. These days I feel quite sorry for those starting out on their career because we certainly have many more obstacles to overcome and you will almost certainly start your career with a not inconsiderable debt burden. Nevertheless, in the true spirit of glass at least half full and by giving yourself a series of short hops on your pathway; you will be able to mark off the waypoints as you make your journey. Fortunately by choosing dentistry as your career, you have picked something which you can be in personal control of more quickly than other more Corporate based careers. We are (most of us) still small business owners or planning to be so.

Hindsight and good luck are great commodities to carry with you (and if you know the secret please let me know), however foresight and good planning are more reliable and I have often felt that those people who you might admire for their apparent success in life have usually generated their own luck by using the 6 P's: **Proper Planning Prevents Pitifully Poor Performance**.

The above paragraph has just reminded me to tell you a little story. Working as a partner in a large mixed practice can be a lonely business. I often thought that all the clinicians would spend lots of time regularly gathered together to discuss the latest exciting development in their sphere of interest. Well no, not really; sensibly they also had another life and encouraged me to do this also. Dentistry is great, but not 24 hours every day.

Anyway back to work! So I got involved in the BDA Section as meetings secretary and set about organising the programme of speakers. Naturally we all tend to gravitate towards our own alma mater and consequently we had a number of speakers from the London Hospital. Luckily I was offered a part time honorary position teaching undergrads in Periodontology and Oral Medicine. I was working with some of the most highly acknowledged people in the field and before long had the opportunity to write my first research paper and having the pleasure of seeing this accepted for publication in a well-known refereed journal. Getting one's name in print (assuming it's not the News of the World) for the first time is very exciting!

I was given more responsibility helping to run the Dry Mouth Radiotherapy Clinic and teaching my own student groups. As I said before I am not the most confident of people and when I started to get invitations to give presentations I found that I needed to 'manage' this carefully. Luckily I had some great advice from my friends at the London and have now given many presentations. I still get slight jitters beforehand and this is good news; the day you don't is the day you don't give a good performance. These early presentations brought me closer to more knowledgeable people and has given me some really great opportunities to develop my practice and broaden my field of knowledge. You notice at the beginning of this paragraph I said 'luckily'? **Actually luck had nothing to do with it**. I knew I wanted more knowledge and I knew the people I wanted to get it from.

Around 2000, our partnership was approached by a small corporate. We saw this as an opportunity to stay in our nice practice and yet re-invest our shares as individuals in other ways. This is the beauty of joining a corporate and because we chose wisely the small corporate kept a good hands off approach to the way we wished to care for our patients. Within two years the small corporate became a bigger one and I had itchy feet to discover what it would be like to start a practice from scratch. I had lots of ideas which understandably would not be what a corporate would necessarily want to try.

After 25 years stability I had decided to stretch myself again and make myself a little uncomfortable. I believe it's good to do this sometimes. Knowledge is power and I made sure I had good advice from people who would also allow me a little latitude to try my ideas as well. Some advisors want to smother you, which didn't suit me. There are many good and some great advisors/mentors out there. But horses for courses and before you settle on one, try a few.

Private dentistry means that patients come to see you, not someone else. It worries me when a dentist buys someone else's private practice and then the patients don't return. I called my new practice Keith Hayes Caring Dentistry, because that is exactly what it was. Nobody wants surgery and what's in a place name? So if you take only one thing from this chapter of mine; consider using your name and caring. We started a few innovative (for 2002) ideas such as a pick up collection and drop back at home service for those without transport, calling patients at home that evening to check all felt fine, coffee and fresh fruit, daily newspaper and local artist exhibitions in the small (2 surgery) practice. The building was quite quaint (beamy) and we had nice oldish comfy sofas and perfumes in the loos. We had the latest high tech in the operatories though with digital intra oral photography, DVD's playing on the ceiling, Diagnodent, soft tissue scanning etc.

I would always personally escort the patient back to reception and often book follow up appointments, take payment and take the time to talk. These are the things that my friends/patients really treasured. We always stocked all the healthcare items we recommended and always undercut the superstores. On one occasion I went to Boots and bought their entire stock of Braun brushes on offer using my Advantage card. I then sold them in the practice at that price and told the patients. They liked that!

Every new patient generated a £5.00 donation into the Keith Hayes Charity Aid Foundation account and patients would 'vote' using coloured buttons into a glass jar (thank you Waitrose) for the charity of their choice. Patients liked that and brought more patients like them. Within 6 months of opening we had 1500 private patients. Between 2002 and 2008 as well as building my practice I was building my knowledge. I believe that you can't have too much knowledge and as soon as you acquire it, it begins to date. Therefore you need to constantly look at refreshing it. There are huge numbers of opportunities these days to do this, but first of all put your ladder against the right wall. Sorry for the cliché, I think it well describes how we can make mistakes and just because we have spent some money on it, keep spending even when it's wrong for us. GDPUK is probably for me the most valuable single resource that I have ever found and guess what; it's free! You can't be an expert in every aspect and therefore once you are up-to-date with the essentials, I urge you to become expert in just a few. This will keep you interested and current and before you know it, others will be asking you.

I developed an interest in Minimal Intervention Dentistry and this lead on to Ozone, caries diagnosis, air abrasion, endodontics, periodontal pocket disinfection and so many other things. I have been all over the world giving presentations on this that and of course the other. But doing this keeps you interested. For me this is the key to improving your practising career and always looking to make the next small step of your journey.

Those of you who know me may wonder why I have not mentioned those three little letters C Q C until the end?

Well the reason is that despite all the bad press, it boils down to just that: Care and Quality and although the CQC expect you to tick all the boxes; it also expects you to understand how you deliver the service and outcomes to your patients, your staff and yes yourself.

Patients want to like their dentist and dentists want to like their patients, obvious isn't it! Not to all though. Take a good look at your practice with a fresh set of number 1 eyeballs and tell me if you like what you see. If you aren't sure that it's what you are proud of then get advice. Shop around and speak to others on what is available. Try out different advisors and see who you are comfortable with. Don't bury your head in the sand and hope it will go away. There is no problem that is too big to solve.

Finally what happened to my Dad? Well I found him again and now I've taken the time to know him, I have found he has a great sense of humour and like me treasures knowledge and also common sense. Unlike me he is utterly confident.

**Keith Hayes BDS**

**Clinical Director Apolline Ltd.**

**www.apolline.uk.com** – The UK's first service company dedicated to providing a comprehensive, individually tailored service to dental practices in all matters relating to regulatory compliance.

# Simon Hocken

**"Denial is the unconscious determination that a certain reality is too terrible to contemplate, so therefore it cannot be true. In the business world, countless companies get stuck in denial while their challenges escalate into crises."**

- Richard S. Tedlow, Professor of Business Administration at the Harvard Business School

When running a dental practice, denial and inaction are very risky strategies! Instead, in order to move their business forward, practice owners need to be aware of their blind spots, deal with realities head-on and take (the right) action.

### Are you One of the Best or One of the Rest?

These days, I spend a lot of time presenting to groups of dentists and their teams. I know that these audiences really like two things:

**Tactics that have worked for others and**

**Success and disaster stories from the world of dental practices.**

It's pretty lonely being a dentist and they want to know what the rest are up to; either to confirm that they are on the right track or to get hold of some new ideas to take back to the practice and try-out.
So far, so good, except most of the ideas never actually get tried out! They sit as notes on paper (or these days on an iPad) providing comfort for the owner who hopes that one day, he might find time to do something with them. They've dropped the ball (the ball being focus, commitment, even success).

Over the years, I've become increasingly curious about what separates the dentists who implement the ideas from those that don't and even why some practice owners are still succeeding when, these days, most practice owners are slipping backwards. So, I want to introduce you to three types of practice owner, examples of which I meet every week. These are stereotypes, of course, but hopefully useful models to help you understand the characteristics of the best and those of the rest.

## 1) The Ostrich (Hope Strategist)

**The Ostrich wants a quiet life.** They may have fallen out of love with dentistry but remain in love with the lifestyle that it has created for them. Very often, they stumbled into practice ownership years ago, as some sort of 'natural progression' from being an associate and these days they often feel somewhat depressed and aggrieved by the increasing demands being made on them such as CQC, HTM01/05, Employment Law etc.

They seek out colleagues who confirm their view that all the fun has gone out of being a practice owner and that the rule-makers are out to get them.

- **They rarely have much hard data** because for many years now, they have been running their practice by: monitoring the white space in their diaries, their bank statements and their annual meeting with their accountants.
- **They are often micro-managers and have a high staff turnover.**
- **Their practice managers are usually low paid ex-receptionists or ex-nurses who have little experience or training to do the job they are now being asked to do.** They often make a competent job of running the operations in the practice, but really struggle with managing the practice's Marketing, Sales Processes and Financial controls, so they don't!
- **The Ostrich know that they need to invest in their increasingly faded and outdated practices but they don't really want to spend their falling profits.** If they did decide

to invest further, they would struggle to know what to invest in except perhaps a new surgery for themselves. However, they tell themselves that although the patient list has got a bit smaller and new patient numbers are falling, the old patients still love them and one day - *hopefully* - it will all get back to the way it used to be. **Essentially, The Ostrich would prefer not to implement any changes...**

## 2) The Enthusiast (Information Gathering Strategy)

**The Enthusiast loves dentistry** and will often tell you that what they really want is to "just do the dentistry". They are great fun to be around because their passion for fixing teeth is infectious! Naturally, they love clinical courses and in their office you will find piles of books, course hand-outs, magazine articles etc, waiting to be implemented. The Enthusiasts spends many hours of the week seeing patients and will fit in running the practice into the gaps during the day. They have made clinical dentistry their hobby and some even visit the practice at weekends in order to fix broken kit.

- **Often, they are sophisticated, highly skilled restorative dentists** and they love clinical courses and trade shows, investing heavily in clinical skills and equipment.
- **They often achieve high gross fees, which quickly disappear in the (high) costs of their practices.** They don't know much about the numbers because in the past there has always been enough money, although these days the overdraft seems to be climbing.
- **Most Enthusiasts are naive leaders**, trusting their teams to do what it says on their job descriptions. In return, their often-loyal teams appreciate their skill sets and will defend them to the last.
- **They talk a lot and change their mind often** and so none of their team really understands where the practice is heading. They are keen to make decisions to advance their practices and essentially, they will implement such changes as soon as they have gathered some more information...

# 3) The Implementer (Driven by Objective Strategies)

**The Implementers are ambitious and have created a clear set of short, medium and longer-term business objectives so as to develop their practices.** In order to achieve these objectives, they have reduced the amount of time they spend treating patients and increased the amount of time they spend working on their practices.

- **They make a lot of decisions**, knowing that some of them may not work out and that this gets things done. They do not get anxious about making decisions.
- **They are not nervous about investing in their practice and they do this willingly once they have quantified the return they can expect on their investment.** This means that their practices are constantly evolving towards their objectives and their whole team is fully briefed on where their practice is heading. They have researched their options (or better still have their business manager help with this) and they have the right information from the best advisors.
- **They have hired a team that is skilful and that can be trusted to do the job on time, on budget and to the right standard.** They achieve this by making very clear requests of their business managers.
- **Implementers are quiet and competent leaders who understand the value of time spent planning.** They always prioritise their action lists highlighting the actions that will create the biggest differences and set time scales to have these actions completed. Their teams are motivated, well paid and willing to go the extra mile.
- **Essentially, The Implementers understand two things: that talk doesn't count, only actions make a difference and secondly, that progress is more important than perfection.**

## In Summary:

What type of practice owner are you? No matter which category you

fall into, I'd be willing to bet that you still want more patients, increased profits and the freedom and flexibility to enjoy your ideal lifestyle. Yet only one kind of practice owner is achieving all this. It is self evident that information, tactics and ideas are of no use to you **unless they get implemented!**
**I have highlighted the attitudes and behaviours that the most successful practice owners exhibit.** Decide on what you want right now. If you want a quiet life, keep burying your head in the sand or continuing to gather information. But denial and inaction won't build a solid business foundation.

## Simon Hocken- Director of Coaching

**www.nowbreathe.co.uk**

For more guidance on running a successful practice, contact the **Breathe Team on 0845 299 7209 or *info@nowbreathe.co.uk***

Choosing the right attitudes and behaviors will be more important to your success than choosing the right tactics.

# Tony Jacobs - Information helps you relax

Picture yourself having a sleepless night, turning over in bed worrying about this or that in the practice, issues with your team, a patient or a government body, knowing that as professionals with our livelihood at stake we have to do the right thing day after day, hour after hour, minute after minute - we know we should run our lives in a careful ordered professional way to prevent this happening. We all know that rules, regulations and things that become customary are constantly changing, and it may be that the rate of change is faster these days than ever before.

This chapter is about my internet forum for dentists, which has the benefit of keeping you very well informed of all that is new and changing. This will help to improve your working life by giving you information, shared by colleagues, and therefore your life will be more relaxed. In addition you will have information that your colleagues nearby may just not have, and this will give you an edge.

The title for this chapter may seem illogical, but it is a serious point, and as this book is about reducing stress in one's life in dentistry, my contention is that the better one is informed, in all fields of dentistry, the more complex issues become simpler.

As a dentist in general practice myself I have learnt ways of controlling the stress that pervades our working lives, and the lives of people working in all sorts of professions. My piece therefore is about the thing which has made me well known in the comparatively small world of UK dentistry, the online forum and community I founded way back in 1997, GDPUK.com. GDPUK is a simple acronym, and don't we dentists love acronyms, standing for General Dental Practitioner - United Kingdom.

The website is for all members of the dental team, and some enlightened people from the dental trade are members too, they learn more about the market they service by have a greater insight into what dentists are thinking and many add value to the discussions by putting forward their point

To give you an idea of the reach of this website, there are around 20,000 dentists in general practice in the UK, and in 2011, around 2500 different dentists log into GDPUK every day, around 14,000 unique visitors each month, and they make about 60,000 visits, creating 2.5 million pages each month. One of the things that makes the forum of the website better is that there is a gateway to access, and people have to be approved to gain access to the site. This means when dentists commence or contribute to a discussion, they know they can write as they are amongst a group of fellow professionals, it is not an open website that can be read by the public. Examples of sites that can be read by the public are newsgroups, Faceboook discussions, Linked In dental discussions and so on. From being in dental school, dentists find they do have things in common with their peers, and discussing those matters helps all parties feel better. The one raising the point feels they have shared the issue and a reader or responder knows that have had the same experience previously.

When I started the group, it was formed as an electronic mailing list, and members were able to post messages to what was called a list server, and this then sent the message out to all the other group members by email. Any member could then reply to any earlier posting, and this way a conversation developed. Some postings would get few reading and no replies, some generate massive interest, with hundreds of replies from hundreds of different dentists, all expressing their varying views, allowing a consensus to form. Sometimes there are disagreements on the way, sometimes full blown arguments when strong willed people take opposite stances, but those types of thread are even more interesting, when the views are so firmly held.

Another way in which I am personally lucky to have started the group, developed it and persisted with it is that this has really changed my life from being in general dental practice fulltime, I can now devote some of my working week to GDPUK. I have become known by colleagues up and down the country have been elected to various plaudits and awards, which are very flattering, and it has allowed me to run courses, meet colleagues at courses, trade shows and dental events. As an outgoing person myself, it is great to know, be known and held in some regard by so many colleagues. GDPUK has also led me to be known in all parts of the dental trade, and I have had a number of regular monthly columns for dental magazines, as well as writing occasional articles for other dental magazines.

I do refer to the GDPUK group as a community and it does compare to any other group of people, imagine a village hall or a British pub, the people gathered will always include many quiet ones, who sit in the corner and keep themselves to themselves, then there are the loud mouthed, the noisy, the witty ones. The village idiot is there, as well as wise person who speaks rarely, but when they do pipe up, it's worth listening. All those types and more are there, every day, on GDPUK.

The GDPUK community has grown from a small handful using email in 1997 to the thousands on the site every day in 2011, and from using a simple email list server, with the aid of dental colleague Steve van Russelt, we have built a website which is composed of many pieces of software working together to make a seamless user experience. The site is free to users, and costs are borne by advertisers and sponsors from the dental trade.

The present site has a forum, which still has a mailing list function, as well as news and comment sections, "ask the expert", image and file galleries, classified ads, dental show reviews. The file section has a function which also fits in with the aim of this book and this chapter, colleagues may place files here of interest to others, and sometimes they are so valuable there will be thousands of downloads of a particular document.

Here is a simple example from the forum of how it all works, in summer 2011. A colleague posted about how a friend's practice had been visited by a "private investigator" working for the GDC, to check if there were any unregistered nurses working at the practice. It turned out there was one such nurse, and she was enrolled on a recognised course commencing shortly. This investigator, who claimed to be an ex-policeman, then asked questions about GDC registrations, and demanded to see all the GDC registration documents of all the team. Colleagues on the forum spotted what was occurring, and all sorts of questions were asked, all of which were educational to other GDPs - this "investigator" had no right to see such information without a court order, sharing that information would be breaching the data security of the employees. Several other breaches were suggested by the visitor, and then doubt was cast on whether the investigator had actually been sent by the GDC at all. This episode gave us many aspects to ponder; it was a real learning experience of the practical aspects of an unexpected visitor claiming to be from an official source, whose mention puts dentists and teams on the back foot.

If I were to refer to my practice, it is possible we could have been caught out by a caller of this nature, but this will now be mentioned at a team meeting, and all will be forewarned, should a similar caller try something on these lines.

This gives you some idea of how a forum works, a forum member may post a question, comment or statement, and this might attract the interest of others reading it. Some posts are made and no-one replies. In this case the initial comment attracted a reply, this then attracted more replies and a conversation commenced. Not every thread is a nugget to every reader, but there is a clear educational experience.

One of the most active threads was from the time of a TV documentary about dentistry in the spring of 2011, "Despatches". This thread had over ten thousand views, and to show you the widespread impact, it had around 300 replies by dental colleagues, and those replies were written by 86 different colleagues. So 86 people felt they were able to join in the conversation and add their thoughts, insert their personal input, publish this for others to read, and they did not have to seek permission or convince an editor it had to be published. Compare this with "letters to the editor" in a national newspaper; they may get some letters but not so many from such a niche group, discussing subjects about which they are truly passionate. Overall the feedback and involvement of dentists, people like yourself, will rapidly convince you what a great resource for UK dentists GDPUK really is!

Very simply, to get the benefits of what you have read in this chapter, visit www.gdpuk.com and register to join the site, you will read the latest news and comments on it by dental colleagues, you will be better informed and therefore your practising life will be better.

**Tony Jacobs BDS, LDS RCS**

**www.gdpuk.com**

# Tony Kilcoyne - When you look in a mouth, what do you see?

Sounds like it's a simple enough question at first and thus it should have a simple enough answer, right? Well I have been learning Dentistry and teaching Dentistry at undergraduate and postgraduate levels for some 30 years, in the UK and around the World and I can confirm others' observations that if you get 3 dentists to look in a mouth you will often get 3 different treatment plans, so why can't we all agree routinely? How can one make sense of this, never mind plan Career development or adopt new ideas if such apparent disparity exists? Why am I asking all these questions and not giving any answers?

Sorry, it's the teacher in me that has learned from other great teachers that learning is a continual process, an intellectual journey if you like and so if one can discover the answers to such questions through OBJECTIVE inquiry and evaluation, one has raised one's intellect to the next level, rather than just be spoon-fed the (hopefully right) answer without the deeper understanding behind it. But today I am going to break that educationalist rule and tell you the Answer to the title's question right now = You see What you Know!

### Yes that's it, a simple answer to a simple question – or is it?

Perhaps if the answer was re-phrased as, **'you Don't see what you Don't know'**, then perhaps it makes a little more sense, in the context of why different clinicians can give different opinions when faced with the same clinical patient's problems, or more significantly, why even the same clinician may modify and change their approach to the same clinical patient's problem over time. Thus hopefully those 3 dentists get to take part in some peer review, listen, evaluate and then 'grow' by sharing their knowledge, experiences and expertise too, so a better consensus can be reached. Dentistry, isn't just carpentry on wooden teeth, it is both an Art and a Science and our knowledge, skills and experiences all change and (hopefully) improve over time too, as do the materials, techniques and systems within which we may deliver that care. Thus our professional learning and development is forever changing too.

## What is it that you know and how do you know it?

For most it's a combination of learning as much of the established theory and one can then through, carefully mitigated, trial and error, further modification, repetition, guidance from 'superior' clinicians and refinement, develop until one improves enough to progress to the next stage of a skill-set. Sound familiar? Such an approach has merits like it's safe and predictable and has a long track record we are all familiar with, but what happens when things change SO MUCH in Dentistry, that the very high intellect we were chosen for in Dentistry (high A-level science grades, very competitive entry and 5 years university education with longer terms that actually were equivalent to 7 years full-time standard university terms) that such changes mean WE must become the researchers and developers on the Frontlines of Dental care?

Another aspect that nobody really tells you in dentistry is that so many things are changing (not always for the better) that the research published in the Scientific Literature is often NOT sufficient to guide every-day decisions by itself and may even be severely limited by protocols, ethics and time-lines to make it only partially relevant to frontline dentistry. Indeed by the time it is published it may already be out of date, so that study following material X is useless because the company stopped making it and launched a 'new' improved X+ etc. Indeed we seem to have a 21$^{st}$ century speed-affliction where even some guidelines issued by the DH or materials/techniques by some Companies may be severely flawed by being rushed-out or unpiloted, that they become in effect 'experimental' trials on the public in all but name!

So as someone who likes to constantly 'improve' what and how I do things, I have suffered in the past from being an early adopter of new ideas and probably have cupboards full of failed materials, equipment and systems that simply didn't live up to the hype, research or the expectations of their initial launches and justifications, so I decided to try and improve upon my previous performance, seek ideas from other respected colleagues and develop what seemed to be the best ways for ME to improve and prioritise HOW I change things, objectively.

So here is my distillation and systematic ABC way of dealing with change-improvements which I've used and continue to improve over the last two decades of clinical and educational practise:

1. Never change more than 25% of what you already know/do annually, unless it has/would cause you a great disaster of some kind. I say this because what most people already do is satisfactory (if occasionally frustrating), so we should build upon that 'level' as a solid Foundation – it also means if something goes badly wrong, fails prematurely, or has unpredictable consequences (financial or clinical), you still have 75% stability and will recover relatively easily, whilst minimising any unintended harm or problems caused. Two obvious examples are changing more than 25% of staff in one go and changing more than 25% of the Labs to try and improve quality/profits - both could be very destabilising for different reasons, yet problems may not be so obvious straight away.

2. As 12 months approaches one can evaluate changes better, keep the good ones, reject the bad ones and from that stable base make further improvements too – thus in only 4 years or so one can move forward relatively briskly and eventually completely change, whilst maintaining stability and reducing risks to the unknown, in a progressive way.

3. Evaluating changes objectively – this is probably the toughest thing to do properly because we are all human, all emotional and despite many years of scientific and logical training, we still have a tendency to bias our decision-making processes, so to help me evaluate introducing something 'new' to the practice, in terms of overall benefits, I created my **KOST analysis**, which stands for Kilcoyne's Optimum Synergy Test. Whatever one uses though, it does need to be objective and using the system below has helped me decide

whether (or not) to spend the time/money/effort on something new and if I go against my 'system' evaluation, at least I know I am making an emotional, rather than a prioritised or logical choice! So here it is and I hope you find it useful too.

## Kilcoyne's Optimum Synergy Test, KOST.

**K** ilcoyne's – Well I couldn't resist putting my name to this, so it reminds me to evaluate WHO does significantly benefit from any proposed change, Patients, Professionals or Bureaucrats? (Does clear advantage pass to those above, compared to previous methods, or not clear?)

**O** ptimum – Does this improve Reliability or Outcomes *without* being too Onerous? (Patient focused, does it reduce errors & increase health without other consequences?)

**S** ynergy – Enhances care delivery by saving time, funding or stress for dental teams. (Does it fit in easily to existing systems & free-up resources to improve other care aspects?)

**T** est – Is it highly evidence based, little/no evidence (experimental)/ goes against EBD? (References - Changes well supported/unsupported by Consort levels of scientific evidence?)

I use this Scoring guide in the table below, keeping it as simple as possible:
+1 each positive, -1 each negative, zero if doubtful, Refereed Evidence = levels 0-3

| Proposed Change | K | O | S | T | |
|---|---|---|---|---|---|
| Score (+3 to -3) | | | | | Out of 12, (+6= viable) |
| total | | | | | |

*Here are 3 different worked examples I used to objectively analyse changes for my practice:-*

## 1. Automated Washer-Disinfectors

| AWDs | K | O | S | T | |
|------|---|---|---|---|---|
| Score (+3 to -3) | -1,+1,+1 | -1,0,-1 | -1,-1,-1 | 0 | Out of 12, (+6= viable) |
| total | 1 | -2 | -3 | 0 | -4 |

K =
- Proteins baked onto AWD instruments is bad for patients so result must = -1
- Prevention of needlestick from unwashed instruments good for dental team = +1
- Good for Bureaucrats so can show pieces of paper for this single stage = +1

O =
- AWDs are relatively complex, unreliable, breakdowns can interrupt care = -1
- Not proven better/cleaner instruments compared to current methods = 0
- More Onerous for Practice, so distracts resources away from current care = -1

S =
- Doesn't save time, increased time of cycles, stages and delays = -1
- Doesn't save funding, costs more initially and in maintenance/extra instruments = -1
- Doesn't reduce Stress, increases things that can go wrong/interrupts flow of care = -1

T =
- No good Scientific Trials to demonstrate benefit, some evidence suggests harm = 0

So overall score is NEGATIVE and doesn't come anywhere near a positive objective score.

## 2. CBCT Radiography

| CBCT | K | O | S | T | |
|---|---|---|---|---|---|
| Score (+3 to -3) | +1,+1, 0 | +1, +1, -1 | +1,-1, +1 | +2 | Out of 12, (+6= viable) |
| total | 2 | 1 | 1 | 2 | +6 |

K =
- Patients get easier access to better 3D diagnostics = +1
- Practitioner gets more information to diagnose with greater accuracy = +1
- No particular effects on Bureaucrats = 0

O =
- 3D Scans reliable and digitally stored for backups and sending to referrers = +1
- Outcomes improved by more information and avoiding complications = +1
- More Onerous analysis and skills than an OPG = -1

S =
- Saves time to take, reconstruct and analyse 3D anatomy = +1
- Purchase costs relatively very high = -1
- Reduces stress by making the unknown, known, method similar to OPG = +1

T =
- Good Scientific evidence for 50x lower dose + improved clarity over CT = +2

So a positive score of 6 overall for CBCT, just reaching viable levels for my Practice.

## 3. Adopting new Resuscitation Guidelines

| Defib | K | O | S | T | |
|---|---|---|---|---|---|
| Score (+3 to -3) | +1,+1, +1 | +1,+1,0 | +1,0,+1 | +2 | Out of 12, (+6= viable) |
| total | +3 | +2 | +2 | +2 | +9 |

K =
- Patients get improved survival rates through AED usage = +1
- Dental Team gets improved logical life support training = +1
- Bureaucrats get consistent training across public&professions = +1

O =
- Reliable ABC and AED system which is applicable in various scenarios = +1
- Improved outcomes by involving AED earlier for diagnostics/shocking = +1
- Involves more training,equipment and maintenance but less drugs needed = 0

S =
- Saves valuable time for diagnostics/shocks whilst paramedics on way = +1
- Costs moderate extra funding initially, but not recurring for 5 years = 0
- Reduces Stress by using AED early, less drugs for easier protocols = +1

T =
- Good evidence base early AED use saves lives + removed unproven drugs = +2

A very positive score of +9 out of a possible +12 maximum in 4 KOST categories.

Thus based on the above 3 worked examples, applying the KOST analysis makes prioritising my Practice changes that benefit patients most, very clear indeed:

**1. Implementing the new Resuscitation Guidelines has high objective benefits overall.**

**2. Acquiring a CBCT machine has viable objective benefits overall, despite high initial costs.**

**3. AWDs for English DH "best practice" has major flaws and doesn't objectively benefit overall.**

Of course legislation or a corporate decision from above may force you to do something which conflicts with your KOST analysis, but those implementing such rules SHOULD carefully consider the overall negative effect upon patient care too, from diverting resources away from treating more people to using poor evidence-based ideas experimentally that may actually be harmful overall.

What is bad for Dental Teams is usually bad for Patients too! A simple KOST analysis can quickly expose weak propositions and PRIORITISE where resources (money and time) could be better spent.

**In conclusion** – The essence of being a Dental Professional means we need to be independently thinking and questioning why changes are needed and be able to justify which changes should be prioritised to benefit patients' best interests in the longer term. The more we know, the more we see and understand, the better care we deliver overall in our dental teams. That was the main point of my original title/question. I hope this short article helps you to be more objective about what you do and don't know, which of many changes to prioritise and which ones to avoid, to help you continually improve as a thinking Professional.

## Dr. Tony Kilcoyne FFGDP, MDDS RCS. MMedSci, LDS RCS, BDS

## www.smilespecialist.co.uk

A Specialist in Prosthodontics at his referral practice in West Yorkshire, an appointed dentist member of the General Dental Council regulatory body, the Clinical Director for the **online** CPD provider 4everlearning ( **www.4everlearning.com** ) and a Dental Foundation Programme Director for the Yorkshire and Humber region ( **www.yorksandhumberdenery.nhs.uk** ), however all information in this article are purely Dr. Tony Kilcoyne's personal opinion alone and is not associated with any other bodies or organisations whatsoever.

# Andy Lane - Clearing the Decks

When Stephen asked me to contribute a chapter to this book on mastering the secrets of successful dental practice I was transported back to the day it all finally clicked into place for me, a day that really signalled my transition from "surviving" to "thriving".

This was the moment, during a lecture from my great mentor Bill Comcowicz, when I came to realise an uncomfortable but inescapable truth: I would never be good at, or enjoy, all aspects of dentistry.

We general dental practitioners often seem to be incapable of admitting that there is some aspect of "general dentistry" that we aren't very good at; it's like admitting you're not a very good driver. It's just too embarrassing to accept for many of us. I will admit, here and now, that I'm really, really rubbish at making full dentures. I've been on lots of courses; tried numerous impression materials and techniques; bought all the right bits of kit, but somehow they are always unstable. It's an art I cannot master.

Equally, there are some things that we just don't enjoy doing. We dread patients coming in who need such a procedure, even if it's our favourite patient, and we will find any excuse to put off providing that thing even though we know it needs to be done. For me this is pretty much anything invasive on a child under 12 years old, closely followed by the surgical extraction of impacted lower 8's. I'll do it, but I'd rather not thank you very much!

Then there are the people you really don't want to treat, or find it difficult to treat because you don't feel sympathy for them or have any empathy with them. It wouldn't matter if they wanted your favourite procedure doing; they're just awful to treat. For me these are the people who don't make an effort to look after themselves or take responsibility for their own problems, and those who are eternally *un*grateful.

You can add into this mix that there are methods of remuneration that some of us are happy with, some we find stressful and some we wouldn't touch with a bargepole. Some of us may be uncomfortable talking about money with patients, and hopefully another chapter in this book will help us overcome that handicap, so we might prefer to work in a salaried service, or on people who are exempt from NHS charges, or be happy to hand the responsibility over to a private capitation provider. Others prefer to be rewarded appropriately for our work, on a fair fee-per-item or time and materials basis, and we wouldn't work any other way.

It is widely recognised that spending even a small proportion of our days doing items of treatment we hate, on people we dislike, under a payment system we find inequitable, can be a source of great stress and unhappiness. It's a wonder any of us put up with this situation year in, year out, but we most certainly do. Working like this was responsible for me coming very close to leaving the dental profession completely within a mere 18 months of qualifying. I was earning a lot of money as an associate attempting to reverse the effects of years of neglect on the dental health of 6,000 of the most unhygienic inhabitants of a Lancashire town the Beatles made famous for the number of holes that needed to be filled there; it certainly felt like I'd filled them all by the time I left, screaming. No doubt they all returned within a short space of time.

To move forward we must learn to accept we can't, or would prefer not to, do everything for everyone. Acknowledging this is an essential step towards developing a way of practising that is less stressful and more satisfying, rewarding and sustainable in the long term.

Let's be honest here; in most practices who is the person that usually decides what we do, when we do it, how quickly, to what standard and to whom? If you're anything like the majority of us GDPs, most of the time this person will not be you.

Uncomfortable as it might be to admit, we're rarely the masters of our own destinies in dentistry; our heads are likely to be down, beavering away on the pressing item requiring our immediate attention at that particular time, tucked away in our narrowly-focussed world, seeking out a fourth canal or refining a margin, surrounded by our materials and paraphernalia. Before we know it days, months and years have passed by.

So, who does really decide how our days and weeks are structured, and which patients fill our appointment books if it's not us? It might be our boss if we're working as an associate or for a corporate; it might be that we have to fit in with "the way it's always been done here"; it might even be our practice manager, but it in all likelihood it will be our receptionist who decides which patients are booked in, for which procedures, at what time, on which day and probably even for how long. And there's another great source of stress right there, the appointment book. How many of us have to cope with too little time, too many patients, too much pressure, too little control, and no space for emergencies or catching up.

So, this is the "default" position for GDPs; we've all been there – it's what happens when we first join a practice and learn to "fit in". We allow ourselves to be pushed along in whatever direction whoever is pushing the hardest wants us to go. It's the line of least resistance, "resistance" being what prevents you changing your situation; the irresistible force that takes you, like a paper boat bobbling along in a stream, ever onward.

Resistance is the enemy of progress. Oh, we feel busy enough keeping that paper boat afloat, baling out, keeping our balance to save it from going under, but any feeling of control is often an illusion. Someday in the future we'll look back upstream and wonder how we got to where we are; it probably won't be where we had imagined ourselves to end up when we became dentists, that's for certain.

Resistance must be fought every single day and conquered anew; even the act of getting out of bed can be hard when you don't look forward to the day and you aren't the one in control of your destination. If you're serious about making life less stressful and more fulfilling, ready to jump out of bed excited about the day to come, you're going to have to take control and paddle upstream or at least across the currents for a while. The good news is that it's never too late.

## The Action Plan

As others in this book will doubtless advise, no goal can be achieved without writing it down. So, please go and find a piece of A4 paper and a pen or pencil.

Your first exercise is to write down every procedure you carry out in dentistry, like this:

- Filling, composite, adult
- Filling, amalgam, adult
- Crown preparation
- Fit fixed orthodontic appliance
- New patient consultation
- Bridge fit
- Surgical extraction
- Implant placement
- Etc, etc., etc.

If you're familiar with Buzan Mind Maps you might find it easier to use one for this exercise, but a linear list like the one above will still work fine.

We then go through the list and rank each procedure from 1 to 5, "1" being the things we love to do, the ones we look forward to doing, that if we had a whole day of these it would make going to work exciting and fulfilling for us. A ranking of "5" is reserved for the things you hate doing, the procedures that if you never had to do another one for the whole of your practising career it wouldn't bother you at all. Everything else is somewhere in between.

We should hopefully find that fitting things (dentures, bridges, crowns, etc.) should be ranked fairly high – if not we might need to ask ourselves some serious questions!

Now please re-write the list again, but in ranked order with everything you scored "1" at the top. If you look at the list now can you imagine how it would feel to only ever do things ranked 1 – 3 and never do the things you have ranked 4 and 5? This is going to be your goal.

There's yet another aspect to this though – the payment system. For the sake of simplicity we will just consider NHS nGDS versus Private Fee-per-Item, but you can apply the same principles to your own variations. So, now decide if you would prefer to see patients as Private fee payers or under the NHS (and you can further refine this to NHS fee-payers and exempts if you wish). You can score this 1 to 3, so let's say we have Private =1, NHS exempt = 2 and NHS fee payers = 3.

Now you can multiply the initial rank (1-5) by the payment system rank and you will find you have 15 possible scores. In the example above all the private treatment will be ranked 1 – 5, NHS exempt 6 – 10, etc. and you can work through your list and refine it further by taking out any items that aren't appropriate, like implant placement or whitening on NHS patients for example.

The next thing you should do is to make a decision about whether there are any items in the list that you can decide right here and now that you will not do, at all, ever, in the future. Cross these items off your list entirely and put these onto a new list of things you will ALWAYS refer in the future. For me this list consists of full dentures and implant placement, which are done by others in my practice, but I know for many this list will include surgical extractions, apicectomies and TMJ problems, but somewhere there will be a person who loves to do those things that you hate so your next job is to decide who that person is – this is really doing your patient a favour because they will be getting an expert who is keen to help, not someone who is doing it under duress.

OK, without realising it you have already made a very big step forward. Unless you are already a specialist this is probably for the very first time you have formally expressed in writing a preference for what you want to do and for what you don't want to do in the future. The next step is to really use the list to change your life for the better and it involves discussing the list with your staff, particularly any nurses you regularly work with, and most especially the person(s) who actually book appointments.

Firstly, give them the list of things you DO NOT DO. Make them swear an oath that, no matter how much you may resist in the future, for your own good they will NEVER allow you to book a patient in for that procedure. You must also compile a list of the people to whom all such cases must be referred in the future.

Now is the time to look at the list of the things you do want to do. You probably need to be sitting with your staff members and have the appointment book open. Work through the list of your priorities and see if they agree with your scoring to make sure you're being completely honest with yourself. If someone walked in needing your very favourite thing, ranked number 1 on your list, how long would it be until they could be seen? For me it would be to start a full mouth reconstruction case and I'd probably want at least 2 hours. If you can say "under a week" that's great, 2 days even better, tomorrow perfect, but if it's more than a week you've got problems – the patient might easily get fed up waiting if they're really keen and go elsewhere. Obviously fit appointments would be dependent upon laboratory delivery times, but again that needs to be as soon as possible. The priority is to never let any of your number 1 procedures get away, ever.

The next thorny issue you're going to have to grapple with is the concept of the "waiting list". Hospitals and almost everyone else in healthcare uses these things all the time but for some reason GDPs seem to find them an alien concept; feeling that they have to fill their books for weeks ahead, no matter what the procedure. In this case less really is more, so I want you to consider how you might use a waiting list to make your appointment system much more efficient whilst at the same time allowing you to shape the direction your practice takes so that it moves more and more towards providing a lot more of your ideal, most enjoyable and rewarding days when you only see priority 1 - 3 patients.

If we go back to the priority list again we can decide with the reception staff which ones on the list will ALWAYS have an appointment made; if you're brave (and busy) this might be priorities 1 to 3, not so busy it might be 1 to 8. Everything else goes on a waiting list, ranked according to the priority system. So, if a patient needs something ranked "15" they're at the very bottom of the list. If you're prioritising 1 – 3 and the patient needs a "4" procedure they go to the top to be called first when a space appears in the appointment book. If you're very brave (and sensible) you will learn to not panic when you see gaps in your book 2 days ahead – this is exactly what we need. If they're still there at the end of the day the receptionist can start filling them up with people from the waiting list, so make sure you have their contact details and they understand that if they turn the appointment down they go back to the bottom of their rank.

Guess what, over time the people who are way down your priority list never get called and either choose a different method of payment (e.g. take the private option) to move themselves up the list, or decide to go elsewhere. Either way you're the winner. Everyone accepts that paying privately will result in being seen more quickly in medicine, so why not apply the same logic to dentistry?

If you have an NHS contract you might be forgiven for worrying that you're being paid to produce a certain number of UDAs and by using the above system be unable to fulfil that commitment. My advice would be to treat your contact as a cheap loan to help you with your cashflow during the transition period and be prepared to pay it back when they ask for it. After all, if that was the way you set your priorities then reducing the amount of time on NHS patients was what you decided was your goal, so enjoy the ride and don't look back! It might be a scary concept, but you really can be self-sufficient, happy, fulfilled, ethical and successful all at the same time.Clearly it's impossible to consider every permutation in every practice in the space of a single chapter like this, but hopefully using these suggestions will give you the basic tools you need to move towards your ideal practice. If you would like to understand more about my approach to practice management I do organise a full range of courses, all inspired by Bill Comcowicz and the rest of the team, at Stockport Dental Seminars. These courses are based on a full and proper understanding of occlusion and how the application of that knowledge within an ethical framework can help you to become the best dentist you can possibly be.

### Dr Andy Lane MPhil, BDS, DGDP (UK)

Dr Andy Lane is the CEO of Private Vocational Training Ltd and the owner of Stockport Dental Seminars. Private VT offers a vocational training for private practices throughout the UK, encapsulating many of the principles offered by the authors of this book with the aim of giving new members of the profession the best possible start to their careers.

Stockport Dental Seminars, originally founded by Dr Roy Higson, has been providing hands-on, practical training for GDPs in occlusion and restorative dentistry since 1982. Uniquely, SDS advanced courses allow dentists to work on their own patients in a supportive, clinical, learning environment with tutors who are real dentists and technicians who practise the methods we teach every day. We believe this to be the best and most reliable way for dentists to transfer their new skills into everyday practice.

Contact: **andy@privatevt.com**

# Ashley Latter

About five years ago I was introduced to a managing Director of an I.T Company, by a dental client and for the purpose of this story, we will call him John. John had developed a superb software application for the Dental Industry and over a short period of time had acquired several clients. My client spoke very highly of John and his product, but he felt his communication skills were holding him back from taking his business forward. After an in depth conversation with John, he confirmed this was the case. He told me that

1.  **He would get nervous before he went into appointments, which would lead to a lot of sweating and perspiration**
2.  **He was a lousy negotiator and he would often undersell his package**
3.  **He could not close the deal and often would have several meetings, but with no conclusion**
4.  **He lacked self-confidence.**

There was more, oh and by the way his average order value was £10,000. For a £995 investment, my two day Ethical Sales & Communication Course would literally solve this guys problems and I would go so far as to say that it would change his life. The other major benefit of taking the programme was that he would also be taking part on the programme with at least 15 other dentists, so he would have a great opportunity to network, build relationships and create more sales. It was a no brainer, the course was great value. John signed up to our London Programme which was taking place in two months time.

About three days before hand, my PA had informed me that John had not sent his paperwork or cheque to us, so I contacted him by telephone. Here is how the conversation went, more or less word for word, after we had concluded the pleasantries.

**A.L** – "John we have not received your booking form and payment"

**J-** "Oh I am sorry Ashley I cannot afford to do your course now, so I need to cancel."

**A.L** – "Oh I am sorry has something happened"

**J-** "Yes we have moved house and it has cost me more that I expected."

**A.L** – "Okay, besides that John is there anything else that causing you not to take part on my programme"

There was a deadly silence for a few minutes.

**J-** "Yes unfortunately I cannot do your course because I hate role play. The thought of standing up saying my name is making me feel ill."

That is what more or less happened. John did not take part on my programme because he was scared about the participation; he was scared of the role-play, not the money which was a side issue.

### Money was not really the issue

The fact that he was scared of the role play was the major reason why he should have taken part. Here is another scenario:

Last year a dentist visited my Exhibition Stand at a major dental conference that was being held in London. He had just heard me speak and was very complimentary about my presentation.
He picked up one of my latest books **Don't Wait for the Tooth Fairy - How to Communicate Effectively & Create the Perfect Patient Journey in your Dental Practice** and started reading it in front of me. He must have been reading it for around 5 minutes (no I am not joking) and then we started talking. He opened up and told me that he had heard of me and complimented me on my courses and went on to tell me that he was hopeless at explaining treatment plans to patients, he talked technical and could not close. He then told me that he was missing out on many thousands of pounds worth of treatment opportunities and this had been going on for a long time now. He enquired about my programme which again, I knew could

have changed his life and after our brief discussion, he said he was going to think about it. Oh by the way he never purchased my £15 book, which told me that he was never a prospect to start off with. If he was not prepared to spend £15 on a book, then he will never spend £995 on a programme. I observed this dentist as he went to another stand and then purchased dental equipment to the tune of £7500. I was gobsmacked.

Here is a dentist whose communication skills were poor, he was missing out on many thousands of pounds worth of opportunities and this had been going on for many years, this had probably cost him many hundreds of thousands of pounds and yet he went onto purchase technical equipment which he will probably never use, or ever achieve a return on investment. What a shame that is.

These are two quick stories, but to be honest; I could share at least a hundred more. Here you have two intelligent guys, probably have superb technical abilities, however because of their poor communication skills; they will never reach their potential. They are probably missing out on thousands of pounds worth of sales every year.

What is apparent to me is that there are probably many possible clients out there missing out on the many benefits that these two Specialists could provide, which is even more frustrating! Yet they don't want to do anything about changing it. In other words, they would rather stumble on, blaming everyone else but themselves, not developing themselves and never reaching their full potential in life. They will go to their grave with a song they have not sung, all because of their poor communication skills.

Okay so I am biased, after all this is what I do for a living, coach people on how to sell and communicate more effectively,  but I honestly believe you cannot spend your money better than developing your Communication & Sales Skills.  Well, maybe you don't see yourself as a salesperson; after all you spent over 7 years learning about Dentistry/Orthodontics, not Communication, or Business Skills.  However, every day you have to sell your ideas whether it be to the patients/clients or to other staff members. If you are not convincing and you are not speaking the language of the person who you are selling to, they probably will not buy into your ideas.

Many studies have been done about what makes a person successful. In fact, here is a simple exercise to do. Think about a person who you know who is successful in Dentistry and develop a list of all the skills, attitudes and attributes that person has. Once you have done this, list them into Skills, Attitudes and Product Knowledge. I bet on the list there are many skills such as, good communication and listening skills, and the ability to build empathy with the patient. On the attitudes side, are there things like positivity and enthusiasm? Have you also got Product Knowledge? On occasions, when I have a discussion with dentists, the technical skills are often left out. Although important and vital, Technical Skills of doing the job, only usually account for about 10-15% of a person's success and without good Communication Skills the ability to build empathy and be able to gain Patient Commitment, you might never be able to put into practice your Technical ability.

## So why is there sometimes negative thinking with regards to the word Sales?

Well, maybe our National Media doesn't help. It seems that whenever we see something in the news about selling, often it is about unscrupulous tactics from salespeople supposedly conning their vulnerable customers. I often think this is unfair, as it is only a very small percentage that might give the many millions of good sales people out there a bad name. If you think about it, without the ability to sell, the whole country would come to a halt and nothing would ever get done. It may also be associated with the assumption that sales is about pushing something onto a customer when they don't really want it. It is hardly surprising that when I ask the question, 80% of the room never consider themselves to be in sales.

## What is the Definition of Sales?

A dictionary definition will tell you that it is to exchange goods and services for money or kind to convince of value.

There is nothing in the definition that states that it is about pushing people or forcing people into decisions. Let us look at another key word here - the word **value**. I think value is about finding out what true value is to the other person in their context, or in other words their situation. So what about changing your mind set from one of selling, or pushing to:

- Building a relationship with your potential client - get them to like you
- Finding out what the patient thinks is value (wants and needs)
- You showing them how you can satisfy them (in a language that they understand)
- When he believes you can, that person will probably buy

If I could leave you with one message from this article it is that developing yours and your team's Communication and Ethical Selling Skills must be a priority. You are all involved in sales in one way or another, every day. Here are a couple of examples; in my opinion the Reception Team are the most important people in your practice. They can make or break whether anyone comes into your building or not by the way they answer your telephone. Whether you are a Dental Practice or an Orthodontic Practice, an enquiry into your practice can be potentially worth £5000. Ensure that your Reception Team have world class communication skills to make this happen, that's why our **Reception Programme – From First Call to Long Term Patient** is so popular. Please visit my website **www.ashleylatter.com** or contact **lissa@thesellingcoach.com** for more information.

Of course there are the Hygienists, who can be major influencers in the Practice. As a side issue, if you have people failing to attend their Hygiene appointments, it is probably because it has not been sold to them properly. Telling the patient that they need to go to the Hygienist for a scale and polish is not a strong enough reason/benefit. It is no wonder, patients fail to attend. It has to be sold better.

Think about it, how many pieces of equipment have you purchased over the years, but you have never really used as much as you should, because of lack of opportunities. How many technical courses have you been on but you have never really had the chance to really put into practice. You can be excellent technically, you can be the best Implant Specialist in the world, but if you cannot sell the treatment or communicate the benefits to the patient, you will never be able to fulfil your potential. That is a shame. Please don't go to your grave with a song not sung.

**Ashley Latter**

**www.ashleylatter.com**

**lissa@thesellingcoach.com**

The leading Dental Business Coach in terms of Communication & Ethical Sales Skills in UK dentistry today. Over the last 15 years, over 5000 delegates have attended his Two Day Ethical Sales & Communication Programme and he delivers this programme all over Europe and in 2011 in Canada for the first time. He is the author of **"Helping Patients to say YES"** and **"Don't Wait for the Tooth Fairy - How to Communicate Effectively & Create the Perfect Patient Journey in your Dental Practice"**.

Ashley writes a newsletter which is read by over 8500 successful business people every month. The newsletter is full of tips and ideas to make you more successful. Please visit his website **www.ashleylatter.com** and register to receive it every month.

# Jane Lelean - The power to change lives by changing smiles

It was a bitterly cold Christmas day 2010, three day old snow had turned to grey ice turning the paths into ice rinks, and the sun had not been seen for days. As I approached the large isolated warehouse complex in East London, it resembled a scene from the black and white photos I saw at the Solidarity museum in Gdansk; small groups of 2 or 3 people huddled around braziers trying to keep warm, checking the passes of everyone who walked by, conducting body searches for drugs, alcohol and weapons. I felt equally nervous and excited about my day ahead, one of the warehouses was a huge cavernous metal shed almost empty except for a dog pound at one end, two caravans at the other, and a makeshift 5 aside football pitch in the middle. How was I to know that by the end of the day I would meet a man that would sing his heart out in celebration and that in his time of greatest need was thinking about how he could improve the lives of others.

So why was homeless man moved to sing on Christmas day?

I was volunteering as a dentist for crises, **www.crisis.org.uk/** a charity that cares for single homeless people. At Christmas they organise centres that are open for six days that offer accommodation food and services that the homeless find it difficult to access at other times such a dental treatment, medical care, hairdressers, clothing replacement repairs, entertainment and much, much more.
As you can imagine providing treatment for homeless is in many ways different from practice, the patients will not be able to return for multi visit treatment plans, and there are often chronic health, and mental health problems, drug and alcohol abuse and trust issues. I had no idea who I would be treating or how they came to be homeless and our remit was not to ask.

I went to collect my patient and was greeted by a smartish man in a wheelchair, who was very angry and resentful that he was at the shelter. He started talking at me about how he had once been an international business man shipping freight all over the world, he had had an accident, broken his back, become wheelchair bound, incontinent and unable to work, lost his income and to add insult to injury had been evicted from his house on the day before Christmas Eve. With no family or friends to support him he started Christmas 2010 homeless and living on the streets in the coldest winters in the last years. Someone found him and drove him to a Crisis centre that opens over Christmas to look after the homeless. He was filled with anger and resentment and yet there was something about him. I was certain there was another quality hidden beneath his anger and resentment and I was curious to find the uncut diamond. I also knew that if I was to have any success treating him I needed to make friends with him first.

In his anger he emphatically told me **"I am not coming back here next year."** To which I replied **"Yes, so what are you going to do?"** he replied giving me the same answer **"I am not coming back here next year"** and I replied **"Yes, so what are you going to do?"** And so this cycle went on, he repeatedly telling me he was not coming back next year and me acknowledging it and asking him what he was going to do. My colleagues were aghast, open mouthed and throwing me disapproving looks that I should not be asking the same question over and over again. And I persisted gently pushing with what I am told is my impish coaching smile that lets me get away with asking what no one else dare and get the answers. Eventually, I got a defiant and different response. **"I am coming back as a volunteer, everyone has been so kind and generous to me I am going to do the same for someone else."** Now my questioning changed and I asked **"What are you going to do now?"** he thought for a long moment and said **"There wasn't a carol service yesterday"**.

Then it began, a single tenor voice resplendently singing the opening bars of the halleluiah chorus, the sound was as crisp and clear as the snow outside had once been and the voice echoed through the empty warehouse as I am sure that the cannons had once done through the streets of Gdansk. My colleagues and I were speechless at the quality of the music that he sang, our hairs bristled and eyes filled with tears of joy. When he finished he said, **"I will start with this, I would** love to have this warehouse filled with people singing and enjoying themselves." As I saw a man who two days previously had been made homeless committed to looking after and bringing joy to others in need, and his anger was transmuted to humility, I uncovered the diamond and it gleamed. In that moment I was reminded of the privileged position I was in, the valuable gift I had been given and why I love dentistry.

Shortly after this I was able to ask what I consider to be one of the most powerful questions that we as dentists can ask our patients, **"What would you like me to do for you today?"** his request was simply, **"Please can you clean my teeth?"** which of course I was delighted to do for him. Not much is as pleasurable as removing calculus that is so thick that you could use it to build a dry stone wall, so satisfying as hearing the chunks of tartar ricocheting up the aspirator and as rewarding as seeing the smile on a patients face when you have made a difference.

Before he left he hugged me and thanked me for all I had done and for making a difference and I replied **"Thank you, you have made Christmas day really special for me too."** Crises is about looking after people, as dentists we spend our working lives looking after others, patients, staff, our families etc. For the most part we are really good at it, and yet how good are we at looking after ourselves?

Consider for a moment your chair, handpieces, your car or any other piece of equipment you use on a regular basis. Imagine that they stopped working, how inconvenient would that be? If your dental chair broke, or your handpieces seized? It would prevent you from being able to work and what problems would that cause you, your staff and your patients? If your car broke down and was going to take a week to fix what inconveniences would that cause? You know that if your important equipment failed it would cause all sorts of logistical nightmares, so you have a service schedule to prevent them. Consider for a moment that you are the most valuable and indispensible piece of equipment in your practice, how well do you look after, service and maintain it? Do you look after your car better than you look after yourself?

Studies have shown teachers that experience burn out and those that don't have different habits of self-care. Those that remain healthy regularly engage in activities that result in them being healthy.

What struck me over the six days I spent at crises is how normal the people were and how improbable it was they ended up on the streets; I met people from a variety of professions including, engineers, ex-military personnel, city traders and a dancer who had been on X factor. Unfortunately circumstances happened that their normal lives changed irrevocable because in some way or other they were not taking care of themselves.

Have you ever considered doing a life audit to see how well you are looking after yourself?

If you are interested, I would invite you to do this valuable exercise today and on a regular basis stopping and reflecting on your life, considering how satisfied you are with certain areas, you can use the balance wheel below. Think of each segment as an aspect of your life and score yourself from zero to ten as to how satisfied you are with each area, join the dots. Below is a life balance wheel if you would like to do a similar exercise for your practice please e mail me jane@healthyandwealthy.co.uk for my 12 spoked dental practice balance wheel.

Now ask yourself:

- **If this were a wheel on a bicycle how comfortable would the ride be?**
- **Is this an accurate metaphor for how you experience your life?**
- **As you look your evaluation of your life are you truly happy with it?**

If you have answered no to the last question I would invite you to consider what would you like your life to be like and what could you chose to do differently that would result in a better experience for you?

Take one area and now ask yourself

- **How would I like this area of my life to be different?**
- **What are some of the many ways that I could make a change?**
- **What resources do you need to implement these changes? This could be help from others, learning new skills, reorganising your time, new equipment etc.**
- **What action are you going to commit to taking and who are you going to ask to hold you accountable?**

Let us go back to our homeless singer who in his greatest hour of need committed to help other people; what lessons can you learn from his story that will improve your life? I would like to share with you what I took away from the experience and the lessons that inspire me daily.

- **Live my life with passion and purpose doing what I love.**
- **Whatever my situation I can make a difference to someone else.**
- **Fulfilment comes from serving others.**

If you are committed to improving your life and practice, I would invite you to spend some time daily, weekly, monthly, quarterly and annually, reviewing your life and setting goals that enable you to spend time indulging your passions and purpose.

**Jane Lelean BDS**

**www.healthyandwealthy.co.uk**

# Kevin Lewis

## Keep the parachute open

As many wise people have pointed out, it is a pity that we spend our whole lives learning important truths, only to fall off our perch just as we begin to get remotely smart in terms of understanding and applying them.

Frank Zappa was an American singer-songwriter and, later, a successful record producer who died in the early 1990s. He is widely credited with the great quote *"The mind is like a parachute – it works best when it's open"* and I was fortunate enough to discover quite early in my career that you shouldn't expect to find all you need to know at dental courses, or within the pages of dental textbooks. So many of those "light-bulb" moments that have illuminated my own thinking have arisen when I was reading things or listening to people a million miles removed from dentistry.

I guess the most profound influence outside dentistry was **Edward de Bono,** who introduced and popularised the concepts of vertical, lateral and parallel thinking. I had been qualified just two years when I read the first of many of his books – I have lost count how many I have read and re-read over the years since then - and nor can I ever bring myself to leave one of his books on the shelf of a bookshop, because no matter how familiar much of the content will be, I know that there will also be a revelation somewhere within its pages that will stop me in my tracks. And I love that feeling. My maternal grandmother was a suffragette, and a lady of admirable determination. I can still hear her voice quietly but firmly reminding me that "There's no such word as *Can't* ".  I was brought up believing that there is no substitute for hard work, determination and sticking to the job in hand and your principles and above all, a positive approach. Everything is possible and every problem can be overcome - even if right now you can't see how that will happen. Giving up was never an option. Little wonder, then, that I felt a huge affinity for de Bono's recurring emphasis on positivity, commitment to purpose and values.

Owning and operating a dental practice in the UK has certainly got tougher, year by year, throughout my professional life and one needs very different skills today to those which saw you through in simpler times. But the same is true of most businesses and sometimes when weighed down with all the legislative and regulatory compliance demands of modern primary dental care we can easily overlook that fact. In very many ways, life in general dental practice is better – or at least, it can be.

Mandatory CPD as a broad principle is an excellent idea and difficult to argue against. But the fine detail as it is currently designed is open to challenge because it drives professional development down very narrow channels. The "core" topics result in rooms being filled with people who, in topping up their knowledge about a small number of topics, no longer have that time available to devote to developing themselves in other ways. There is a finite limit to how much time and money most dentists can or will devote to CPD, and my fear is that fewer and fewer dentists will have enough time or energy left to seek any enlightenment outside dentistry, dental publications and dental courses. And that would be a huge lost opportunity.

Another problem is that, outside the "core CPD" and "recommended CPD" topics, course organisers know that they competing for what is left of the profession's time and money in very difficult economic times. The commercial reality is that course organisers will then look to those alluring, money-earning topics to put bums in seats make their courses viable, and instead of seeking out courses on new, different and unfamiliar topics, the same dentists will keep returning to more and more courses on the same or similar topics.

Edward de Bono describes vertical thinking as digging the same hole deeper, as opposed to lateral thinking in which one starts digging a new hole in a different place. No prizes for guessing which approach is likely to yield the greatest rewards. For me, the stimulation has come from reading a book or listening to a speaker on a topic far removed from dentistry, and recognising the applications for dentistry, or for your practice, or your life. The challenge for me has then been to drag my wandering brain back to the book (or the speaker), once something has sparked a train of thought.

I have been incredibly fortunate in having had such a varied professional career, and the opportunities to indulge all those things in my professional life that I find fulfilling. But many of my colleagues have also found different outlets for their own energies which serve the same purpose. Most of those who have remained the most motivated, for the longest, have had a balance between the four walls of their surgery and something beyond that.

I don't actually think it matters too much whether that "something else" is something away from dentistry altogether, or simply a different part of dentistry like dental politics, or dental education - or even some kind of advisory or consultancy work. But if it refreshes you, re-motivates you and brings you into contact with other interesting and equally motivated people to keep your professional pilot light burning, so much the better. I learned quite early in my career to avoid negative people, because they tend to squeeze the last drop of pleasure out of whatever you do. Instead, surround yourself with interesting and positive people and maintain a sense of balance – and a sense of humour.

## Treat people, not teeth

Theodore ("Ted") Levitt was one of the architects and godfathers of marketing as it is understood and practised today. He argued that many businesses fail to see their product through the eyes of the customer because they are too internally focused. The more specialised and technical the business, the greater the danger that this will be so, and he advocated understanding the business that you are (really) in rather than the one you think you are in. He famously observed, at the time when the US railroad giants were forced to give way to the airlines – not just in terms of passenger traffic but freight traffic also – that

*"The railroads collapsed because they thought they were in the railroad business, when in fact they were in the transportation business."*

I can still remember how I felt when I first read this sentence. It was a marketing book, not a book about dentistry, but it was as if this writer had just shown me where to find the Golden Fleece. There is a massive lesson for dentists in this statement. Many dentists and dental practices seem to believe that they are in the dentistry business, or the tooth business, or the implant or veneer business. In fact they are in the people business, and people buy people, long before they buy veneers from them. The most successful dentists treat people, not teeth.

During the four decades that I have spent in and around dentistry, a number of different factors have combined to have a profound impact on the patient: dentist relationship. Some of it has been self-inflicted (like our increasing willingness to commoditise dentistry and behave as if we were in the hurly-burly of the open market instead of members of a healthcare profession). But much of it has been the result of deliberate policy decisions on the part of successive Governments.

Dentists had traditionally enjoyed a special "relationship monopoly" with patients, which over the years had left Government powerless to control the cost of NHS dentistry. The NICE guidelines to cut the historic public dependency on the "six monthly checkup", the abolition in England and Wales of continuing care and registration, the active encouragement of "walk-in" Dental Access Centres and other more subtle changes had progressively unpicked the threads that had bound the patient and their dentist together for a quarter of a century. My career as a full-time practicing dentist was already over by the time we had specialist lists in the UK, and the NHS-driven concept of "Dentists with Special Interests" came even later. But this additional layer of secondary care also has the potential to change the dynamic of the gdp: patient relationship. The briefest of glances across to the experience of our medical colleagues should be sufficient to warn us of the real dangers of any weakening of the patient: dentist relationship. All the evidence points to the fact that risks increase when patients are treated by people that they have not met previously, and patient trust and satisfaction levels are greatest when a solid relationship has been allowed to develop over time.

Most businesses would kill for the kind of enduring relationship that most general dental practitioners have with their patients. Why on earth would we want to give this away without putting up one hell of a fight?

Another dimension of that relationship is seen in the drivers for patient satisfaction and dissatisfaction. Patients have a limited ability to measure the clinical / technical quality of the treatment they receive, so they tend to use "proxy" measures such as the way their treatment is delivered in terms of their interpersonal experience with the people they deal with on the front desk and in the surgery.

As my career came full-circle with the second half of it being spent in the dento-legal field, I suddenly came to realise – in another "light bulb" moment - that treating people as you would wish to be treated yourself, and building up a really good rapport with them wasn't just a sound business /marketing strategy – it was by some distance your best protection against being sued or on the wrong end of a complaint too. How lucky is *that*? And how sad it is that Ted Levitt passed away before we could give him a "lifetime service to dentistry" award. Perhaps if we just heed his advice, it will be reward enough.

## Kevin Lewis - kevin.lewis@mps.org.uk

Kevin qualified from The London Hospital in 1971. He spent 20 years in full time general dental practice and 10 further years practising part time. He became involved in the dento-legal field in 1989, firstly as a member of the Board of Directors of Dental Protection, then (1992) as a full time dento-legal adviser and since 1998 as Dental Director. He became a member of the Council (Board of Directors) of the Medical Protection Society in 2003 and is a member of the senior management team of MPS.

For 25 years from 1981 to 2006, Kevin was the Associate Editor of *Dental Practice*. Since 2006 he has been the Consultant Editor of *Dentistry*. He has written two textbooks on dental practice management. He writes and lectures regularly all over the world.

# Brian Lux - Patient Meetings

Communicating new ideas, materials and techniques to your patients is easier these days with the ban on advertising lifted, but I wonder how many dentists rely on magazines, constantly running videos in the reception area, and the use of intra oral cameras. There is one area that is neglected, and that is meeting your patients in a neutral area to discuss dental topics, and have a good question and answer session.

I cannot recall any report of one except my own, and that was thirty plus years ago when any attempt at advertising would result in a summons from the GDC, and a possible appearance before the Disciplinary Committee. But I did run, not one, but a number of meetings successfully, resulting in a greater uptake of private treatment, and-I hope- a better understanding by my patients of the complexities of dental problems and their treatment.

### So how did I do it?

We had a practice discussion to decide on the venue, numbers we could accommodate, refreshments, invitations, security (to ensure only patients attended), and the format of the meeting. Luckily a new hotel nearby was in the process of opening, so I arranged an appointment with the Manager to discuss the meeting.

My first victory was to be offered space for no charge, as he felt the meeting was good for promotion. We then agreed a price for visitors to be offered a glass of red or white wine, with some cheese nibbles, as I felt it important to offer some light refreshment, and commend this strategy. A date was fixed (after seeing what was on the telly that evening), and now came the task of advertising the event to the practice.

These were the days before the computer, and I used a local secretarial service to address the hundreds of envelopes needed, and a local printer produced copies of my invitation letter plus (the most important writing) the entrance card.

I guessed that as news of the forthcoming event circulated, I would have hostility from local practices, and it was imperative that no interlopers could gain admission. Patients who wished to come could apply in person, or by telephone for tickets, with no charge, of course. A list was compiled, and each admission card had the name of the attendee filled in at the practice, so that on the evening of the meeting, card names were ticked off against our list. **No card, no admission.**

That vital check was to prove important in view of a subsequent letter from the General Dental Council. The format of the meeting was finally decided by myself, and now it just needed the blessing of the Medical Defence Union, to which I sent a copy of the invitation letter. '**I am disappointed to find a member who is quite so determined as yourself to place his head on the chopping block,**' began the letter from the Dental Secretary, who then continued to challenge some of the contents, especially in relation to my comments about the NHS and child dental caries.

Unfazed, the preparations continued, and I was delighted at the number of applications. The atmosphere was convivial, relaxed, and by having a member of staff at the door, only bona fide patients entered the meeting room, though it did not stop hotel guests trying to join in, nor friends of patients who came with them, but all were politely refused admission. Even the local press were barred when they turned up.

I had planned a talk, illustrated with slides, and an exhibition on various tables, showed crowns, bridges, stages of making a dentures, and the new sensation, brought from the USA, fissure sealing. That technique, with its intense light, proved popular as patients used it on extracted teeth, set in plaster bases. I painted the liquid sealant in the fissures, and patients were able to test the hardness, after they had used the light.

As I was a recent member of the American Society for Preventive Dentistry, I was enthusiastic about tooth brush design, dental floss, fluoride mouthwashes etc. After my presentation, there followed a long and interesting Q & A session, and I was humbled when one patient stood up and asked for a vote of thanks from my patients for the effort I had made to bring them the latest techniques available. At no time did I try and sell anything, nor suggest I had more skills than local colleagues, but the GDC would think otherwise!

At the meeting was a dental technician friend of mine and at the next one he was to play a very important part, which he enjoyed, and I took pleasure in seeing my patients realise that behind my efforts were a team of extremely skilled men and woman whom they never met. The second meeting, six months later, saw Tony set up a furnace in the middle of the room, and after my presentation, he was surrounded by amazed folk as he transformed a mixture of powder and distilled water into a beautiful, life-like, porcelain crowns. His stock soared that evening, and the fixed beaming smile showed how much he enjoyed being centre stage. How many dental technicians ever meet their clients, and how many dentists accord them the respect they deserve, when a grateful patient coos their appreciation for an aesthetic crown or bridge replacement?

At another meeting, a well known dentist, who still teaches correct posture, asked if he could come and report the event, and afterwards, I remember him coming up to me and saying it had given him a lot to think about. As I recall, his report was supportive. I was happy, my staff had been brilliant and enthusiastic, and only positive reactions came from the practice, then a letter from the GDC arrived! Before the meeting I had discussed the idea at the GDC and was told there would be no objections, in principle, as long as I ensured

1. **Attendance only to bona fide patients.**
2. **Subject matter be educational and not advertising any special skills.**

'**The Council has recently received information which suggests that you may be permitting persons to attend the seminars who** are not already the patients of your practice. **If this is so, it alters the whole position and, as you will appreciate, you could be held to be advertising or canvassing for patients.'**

The most stupid objection came when referring to a dental technician being involved. **'Finally, it is alleged that in the course of the seminars a dental technician carries out demonstrations of various *advanced techniques:* (my italics) on the basis of my information taken at its face value, this could be interpreted as extolling the services which your practice can offer, and could thus constitute advertising.'**

However I did like this comment: **'The very fact of the idea's novelty does, however, lay it open to criticism by colleagues *who may be less progressive in their outlook.'*** (my italics) How true, and I was not surprised that local 'colleagues' had taken umbrage at the success of the seminars and lodged formal complaints with the GDC, which is why we had taken such care in the planning stage. My reply was short: prove the charges that

a) **I allowed none patients to attend.**
b) **I never advertised my skills as exceptional.**
c) **The dental technician demonstrated no advanced dental prosthetics, only a porcelain crown, provided by any general practitioner.**

The reply was equally short, and said no further action would be taken, but I must ensure I complied with GDC guidance at all times. Discussing the seminars and GDC involvement with local colleagues was interesting as all were horrified that anyone should have tried to get me into trouble, but my 'Judas' was among them. Today, I suppose you could place an advert in your local paper for a meeting, and I have no problem with that concept, as long as you do not suggest to your audience you are better than the practice down the road. Is the cost justified? If you mean in terms of selling more advanced (lucrative) dental procedure, I can't answer. If you mean in terms of your image as a caring dental practitioner, then you will reap the benefit. But you will enjoy the evenings as much as I did, and shouldn't we have some fun from being a dentist as well as the hard work and increasing frustrations from the bureaucracy?

## Brian Lux

**www.brianlux.co.uk**

**brian@luxb.freeserve.co.uk**

# Bruce Mayhew - Delegate.

Delegation is about giving authority but not abdicating responsibility

For years, I found dentists frequently moaning about how much work they have on their plate. Two of my local dentists have recently thrown in the towel well before retirement because, as far as I can see, they have allegedly been ground into submission. I wonder how many dentists, all over the country, have given up before their time. The job has become too laborious and repetitive compounded by the endless and overbearing compliance and governance. The bureaucrats are squeezing them, looking over their shoulders, breathing down their necks, until eventually and inevitably and with great relief they have said "**No more, I have had enough**".

With GDC, CQC, H&S all adding to the administration, coupled with the draconian employment laws absurdly in favour of the employee, who can blame them?

Too often I hear dentists say they are overworked and are unhappy with their income.  Dental nurses who are bored, therapists and hygienists out of work – it's not just dentists, it's the dental industry.

I believe employing the right staff, motivating, incentivising and then delegating, is the answer to many of these problems.

Delegating the things we are not good at or don't enjoy can be the answer to increased work enjoyment and dare I say it, increased profit. For in my book the epitome of a good dentist is one who does excellent work, enjoys it  AND makes a good profit and if any one of these ingredients is missing then in my opinion they are not a good dentist.

There are thousands of jobs around the practice which dentists insist on doing themselves but fundamentally resent because it's not what they were trained to do, it's not why they entered the world of dentistry and they feel it has no impact on the bottom line - so is it any great surprise they are less than proficient at doing them?

By gaining a greater understanding of your staff's skill sets, coupled with gaining a thorough understanding of their strengths and weaknesses you put yourself in a much stronger position to confidently allocate authority to someone who is going to undertake that particular task with more enthusiasm and vigour than you could possibly muster.

Additionally, if only dentists would realise that selling dentistry takes time (and time is money) and can be done often far better by a member of staff. The staff member, however, needs to understand key elements of dentistry, which means an investment of your time. They need the knowledge and confidence to communicate with a patient in a concise and methodical way, that is jargon free. By committing to this, you are empowering a patient to make an objective and informed decision about their dental care. When this is done well, the patient will want the treatment and will pay the fee with gratitude and appreciation - this should be our aim.

Explaining treatment ideally needs to be done away from your room, (try not to use the word surgery) and away from other patients. For most people this 'selling', for that is what it is, needs guidance and training. To supplement your own training, fortunately these days there are endless excellent courses on selling dentistry. Colin Hall Dexter was my mentor and was the Master but sadly he is now retired.

When the nurse shows the patient in for treatment there is the obvious function of ensuring the patient is at ease, making sure they fully understand what is going to happen and managing their expectations. This importantly includes making sure the fee that has been quoted is acceptable followed by checking the medical history. She can apply a surface anaesthetic and then take the time to reassure the patient and explain how the whole procedure will be utterly painless. After the anaesthetic is completed by the dentist the nurse can apply the rubber dam, fully explaining why it is desirable.

During this the dentist has a number of options which may just be a quick cup of tea or alternatively see another patient in an adjoining room or discussing something with the secretary or seeing a patient in the hygienist or therapy room. It is important to factor this time in, so the dentist has the time to offer the personal touch to a patient's experience.

In my practice nearly all the adult patients are seen by the hygienist or therapist and have IOH and S&P and radiographs (which were prescribed at the previous visit) and extra time is allowed for me to do their examination and check the radiographs. This extra time allows the hygienist or nurse to fully explain any treatment required and fees....no rush, which is so important when running a private practice and something the patients appreciate and frequently comment upon.

Taking the impressions, casting models, making whitening trays and fitting them can all be done by a competent dental nurse. All this together with a full explanation of the pros and cons of whitening is so important for the patient and for the reputation of the practice.

Learning to take photos with a good SLR camera is all part of work enjoyment and increases work satisfaction and is such an important aspect of a dental nurse's job. Showing the pictures to the patient is an effective visual representation of what issues and challenges they face and in our experience can be extremely effective. It's surprising what patients notice about their mouth when they see it on the screen. As with photographs, the taking of radiographs, processing them, explaining them to the patient, helps us show patients that they have teeth worth looking after. In fact why not have an X-ray machine away from the surgery thereby freeing up the dentist's expensively equipped room. If a ledgy filling shows on the radiograph then the nurse can discuss this with the patient and they can decide whether they want to live with the uncleansable ledge or have it eliminated

And lastly, delegate all the admin to a secretary. The single biggest mistake of my career (51years) was working for so many years without a secretary. They do all those things which have to be done of an administrative nature, wages, paying all the bills...work and home, keeping an immaculate spreadsheet of the whole practice workings, making the estimation of efficiency and profits a doddle. Mine also drafts detailed letters to patients with photos and radiographs, fully illustrating the anticipated/completed work as well as information reiterating the discussions already taken place in the practice.

In my practice incidentally, I have on my desk, on the first of each month, a series of figures including the previous month and year to date which help me analyse trends. These figures are gross income, gross expenditure, profit and %, my income, therapist income, hygienist income, days worked for each, hourly gross for each, sessions fully booked ahead and number of new patients (the last two are a good yardstick). This I have had for 25 years now so it is easy to see in a recession if anything is sliding!

Lastly, delegate those things that you don't enjoy or you feel can be done better by someone else but can't be done by your staff. In my case I refer to other dentists for Implants, Endodontics, difficult extractions and orthodontics for children and difficult adults.

### Bruce Mayhew LDS RCS, DGDP

He has practised Dentistry for 50 years and is a Single handed practitioner with 8 staff including a full time therapist and hygienist. He believes a dentist should lead a team and each do what they are competent to do and what they enjoy and refer the rest.
Over the years he has lectured on Practice design, Prevention, Profitability, 4-6 handed dentistry and Practicing clinical dentistry efficiently.
He was President of the UK International College of Dentists for 7 years, Postgraduate teacher for 20 years and Constable of Hungerford for 4 years.

### www.brucemayhew.co.uk

# Paul Mendlesohn

I first heard about Transcendental Meditation or TM, when I was a dental student at San Francisco University. I had been able to take three months off from Kings College Hospital during the last year of dental school for an elective study. I was even fortunate enough to obtain some funding to help with travel and accommodation. I took part in some very interesting projects in San Francisco such as providing gold inlays to medium security prisoners at San Quentin prison and working in mobile children's clinics in San Jose. The gold inlays were produced by a direct technique using small pellets of soft gold burnished into buccal cavities under rubber dam. It was a slow laborious technique that produced beautiful fillings that could last for years.

In the days before cheap flights it was unusual to be British in California and the American patients used to ask me some very naïve questions. One parent said to me "you have a funny accent where, are you from?" I replied "London" and she said "how long have you been here?" I said '"two weeks" and she replied "gee you learned English quickly!"

It was in the 1970s and the Beatles had been spending much of their time with TM's founder Maharishi Mahesh Yogi, which made him a household name at the time. People were meditating in the parks, on public benches and in groups at the campus. I didn't know what it was, but decided to investigate on my return home.

I used to feel quite stressed when working in the clinic and was tired at the end of the day. Whilst this was helped by numerous pints of beer in the student bar every night, I wanted a healthier way to have more energy and feel relaxed.

I found a local TM centre in North London and paid £25 to learn, which was the student rate at the time. I remember going to the pub after the first of three follow up meetings and wondering with the other students if we had spent our money wisely!

The first experiences of meditation were that my mind seemed to become quiet, there were less thoughts and I felt some inner stillness. It's quite subtle at the beginning but it is restful and I felt refreshed and calmer after mediating.

I quite remember when I went back to the dental hospital the first day after learning. I had a happy feeling for no reason other than I felt good. The day in the clinic just seemed to fly by. But when you first learn to meditate, you don't know if the good feeling is related to the meditation or just a positive variation in mood. You are told when learning to just keep meditating regularly for three months and then judge how you have been overall, during that period.

Fortunately the positive feelings continued, my energy levels increased, I was happier, more relaxed and focused. I definitely went through a personality change, I took up sports for the first time, became interested in art with my initial attempts expressed by punk style collages and paintings enhanced by the generous use of glued-on safety pins. During university I lived with four other dental students in a house, they are still some of my closest friends. Within a few months of learning TM they all commented on how I had changed, but perhaps less positively on the punk art that was springing up around the place.

I continued to mediate regularly throughout the last hospital year, twenty minutes twice a day, in the morning before breakfast and in the evening before dinner. I found that the morning meditation woke me and set me up for the day and the evening one dissolved the stress and fatigue that has built up from study and clinical work at Kings.

Soon after qualification I bought my first practice, it was an NHS expense sharing partnership in Holborn London. Even on the first day I couldn't believe how stressful I found it, I was still nervous about giving inferior dental blocks, never mind carrying out posterior endodontics or multiple crowns and I still wasn't used to the fact that there was no demonstrator to check what I was doing and give me advice.

But in the evening when I meditated, the stress of the day dissolved and I felt much calmer and refreshed. On the second morning of practice ownership, I woke up and thought "oh no, I don't think I can do it", but after meditating I felt completely different – I had my 'can do' attitude back.

During the first six months of practice I had a difficult time, dealing with the business aspects that I knew little about, and learning to do dentistry efficiently under the NHS. But over the seven years that I ran the Holborn practice, I found that the TM really helped me, keeping me level headed, energetic and enthusiastic. If there was a bad day when things went wrong, as they invariably do, I felt better after the evening meditation. I also started to enjoy some long-term effects. It is claimed that Transcendental Meditation develops creativity, spontaneity, efficiency and intuition and I felt that these qualities were increasing. I tend to have my best ideas after meditating, when my mind is clearer and calmer. Most businessmen call this 'gut feel' what this means to me is a calm objective view, seeing the bigger picture without the mind being clouded by too many thoughts.

When I started the Whitecross chain with one practice it felt like a natural step, based on 'gut feel', it was a completely innovative step. It was the first branded dental chain, the first to raise venture capital and to float on the stock market.

Maharishi Mahesh Yogi says that happiness comes from growth, from personal progress, that it is not something you reach in any point of time. This has been my experience, that as the years pass I am more dynamic and enjoy expanding my sphere of experience and influence. It's interesting that as my activity become more effortless, I am able to do more, to achieve more with less effort. That's how I was able to be the first to open a chain of 45 branded Whitecross dental practices from scratch.

After more than thirty years of meditation, I find it still helps me on a daily basis and I continue to benefit from the rest and creativity it gives me.

Transcendental Meditation is a simple natural technique, which is practised for 15-20 minutes twice each day sitting comfortably with the eyes closed. The deep rest to the mind and body releases physical and mental stress, which decreases performance, harms relationships, and creates physical wear and tear. In short, stress curtails enjoyment of life. Furthermore it tends to build up in the system over the course of a lifetime. Even a good night's sleep or an extended holiday does not enable us to recover fully. Nowadays, stress is a fact of life - but it need not be.

Mediators say that Transcendental Meditation contributes to more successful and fulfilling relationships, and increases one's ability to give more, in a positive way. It develops a more mature and tolerant personality. It develops broader awareness, greater happiness, and refined feelings and emotions. All these result in a more positive and warm personality capable of enjoying deeper relationships and a richer personal life.

People often ask me how I find the time to meditate as I am always running a number of businesses, manage to fit in lots of holidays and have a good social life. Being Chief Executive of CODE is very complex and demanding job, which means that I usually work all day and many evenings, plus some weekends. However I find that the time spent on meditation makes me more efficient, energetic and effective. It's a good investment in time. The few minutes I spend every day taking care of myself increases my capacity to respond to the needs of family, friends and colleagues. Maharishi says that "The best way to help others is to first help oneself."

There is a fundamental principle of life found in every culture throughout history - "**As you sow, so shall you reap**". It is always true that if we are more positive and open towards others, they reciprocate by becoming more open and positive towards us. In this way, the inner development brought about by Transcendental Meditation is reflected in more rewarding relationships of every type - business, family and social.

Learning to meditate is easy. It's an effortless technique and anyone can do it. You don't need to have any particular skill, there is no special diet or rules to follow and you don't even have to believe that it will work. I often hear people say that they can't quieten their mind so they won't be able to meditate, but I answer that there is no need to make the mind quiet or still, the meditation achieves that naturally.

If you think that TM is of interest to you, I recommend that you learn at an official centre, which can be found at the UK website www.t-m.org.uk . Not all meditation is the same so it's important not to use one of the many copycat organisations. The technique I practise and recommend is the one brought to the west by Maharishi Mahesh Yogi and is taught by his trained teachers at the official centres.

Dentistry is a stressful profession and the role of practice owner or manager is particularly tough. Many colleagues suffer from professional burn out, some from alcohol problems and some from the effects of stress. The research and my experience shows that this simple technique can contribute to a healthy, happy professional career. The best business advice I would give to any dentist or dental team member is to be more relaxed and effective through the regular practice of Transcendental Meditation.

## Paul Mendlesohn, CODE Chief Executive

CODE is the association for dental practice owners and mangers. To find more information about CODE visit **www.CODEuk.com** or call **01409 254354**.

# Barry Oulton

Our brief for this book was "how dentists can improve their working lives". Far be it from me to tell you, the reader, how to improve your working life. I can, however, recommend five occasions that shaped, improved, and influenced my dental life and my personal life too. There are countless examples in fact and so it's been a struggle to limit it to just five. I am not the only one these have worked for.

## 1. Have a mentor, and then become one – with this philosophy we can grow one another and our profession.

For more than 15 years I have been lucky enough to have a brilliant man mentor me. I worked as an associate for Dr Julian Perry in London for 3 years. It was not long after my VT year and I was inspired by his drive, ambition, and commitment to quality and service. JP has done it all – owned and run a corporate body, owned and run 6 successful private practices. He is currently the CEO of a large Body Corporate.
JP has continued to guide me over the last 15 years and still does.

*My Advice – get a mentor. Choose wisely; find someone who is achieving what you want, in the way that you want, with similar values and qualities. Most importantly – mentor someone else and pay it forward.*

## 2. Get Business Coaching – take advice

University teaches us to be clinical dentists. Arguably not very good clinical dentists until we 'learn' in practice. We are not, however, taught to be business owners. I met Chris Barrow in 1998 and was a client of his for over 4 years. I brought my first practice in 1999 and with Chris' guidance and advice, grew it from a run down NHS practice with unhappy patients and staff, into a successful private practice with happy loyal staff who have been with me for over 10 years, a loyal client base and a profit three times the original. This was achieved on 3.5 days a week. Having a business coach also gave me a community of like-minded friends to talk to, share highs and lows with, and bounce ideas off.

*My Advice – get a business coach – choose one with a proven track record of success. Ask around and look for testimonials from practices that impress you.*

## 3. Wind Assisted Extractions!!!

I was a student at Leeds Dental Institute. It was our first week on oral surgery clinic and nervously our first 'hands on' day with patients. Miss C is not only attempting her first palatal infiltration but Mr. Strict oral surgeon decided that it's time for her first extraction – upper right 6. All of our hearts were beating. If I'm honest we also felt better knowing that we were not in her position.
Push – said Mr Strict, push harder, he commanded. Miss C did what she thought she ought as a bead of perspiration appeared on her brow.

HARDER said Mr Strict, PUSH HARDER, he bellowed. Miss C did and at that moment of perspiration and effort...farted like the wind section of the philharmonic!!!!
We, of course, doubled up in laughter. Mr Strict, slight of hearing, continued to 'encourage' Miss C to the point of extraction...

*My Advice – Dentistry can be tough but it's often fun and enjoyable*

## 4. Learn NLP – Neuro-linguistic programming

This, above all else, has changed both my working and personal life, although as with most dentists, it's difficult to separate the two as they are so closely intertwined. NLP was discovered in the 70's and has been researched and developed since then. Learning NLP offers me tools for improving my relationships, parenting my children, developing my businesses, Sales, customer relations and understanding myself. NLP helps me do what I am already doing and to do it even better.
I learnt my core skills with OPAL – Dr Michelle Rhodes

*My Advice – Learn about NLP from a great trainer - visit the Opal website www.opaltd.co.uk*

## 5. Attend a Sales Training Course

I was one of the first 2 dentists in the UK to attend a sales training course specifically designed with the dental profession in mind. The course was great; it blew me away and revolutionised my practice at the time. Some elements of the process, however, were awkward, forced, and made me feel uncomfortable. A couple of years ago I realised why. The course was written and designed over 50 years ago. It delivered advice and teachings based on what was known at that point in time.

Since the time it was written a greater understanding of the human psyche has evolved, not least with NLP. We now know how people 'tick', how we make decisions and what creates our feelings/perceptions and how to positively influence people for the betterment of them and us.

12 years on from that first UK Sales course, Rhodes Oulton Innovations have developed 'The' Sales Training Course for health care professionals incorporating the very latest in understandings about communication, rapport, and service. Proven strategies to discover what your customer/patient wants and how to satisfy them at a deep level.

This is a training course that not only improves the bottom line of a business but also ensures customer satisfaction and retention.

*My Advice – Visit Rhodes Oulton Innovations (www.rhodesoulton.co.uk) to see what delegates are saying about our courses.*

## Barry Oulton BChD, DPDS

## www.rhodesoulton.co.uk

NLP sales training for the dental team

# Dr. Ellis Paul - Prevent Stress, work in Perfect Posture

Musculo-Skeletal Pain, principally in the neck and back is extremely prevalent amongst dentists. Statistics show that 85% of dentists suffer from such pain. The same applies to nurses, therapists and hygienists. It is cumulative and can eventually result in permanent damage which is irreversible. Moreover musculo-skeletal pain also depresses the quality of our work and has a dramatic effect on the quality of life.

## Why do we get Pain?

The major cause in dentistry is almost always from sitting and working in a poor posture. Much dental work involves a high degree of precision and the need for good vision and access. Dentists and other dental workers tend to bend their backs, overflex and twist their necks and raise their arms and shoulders. Any one of these distortions causes pressure on nerve roots producing pain. Over a long period of time this overstresses muscles and ligaments and causes muscle spasm.

In the long term distorted posture causes uneven pressure on inter-vertebral discs. This may cause the disc to bulge and put pressure on nerve roots, which in time can cause referred pain. In extreme cases permanent damage to the discs can occur causing disability, inability to work and, in extreme cases, the need to give up dentistry completely. One problem is that such pain seems to be universally accepted by the dental profession as a fact of life. This is entirely wrong as it can be prevented by working in perfect posture.

## But what is perfect posture?

To work in perfect posture it is essential that the patient lies totally flat so that the frontal plane of their face is parallel to the ceiling. To this end the dental chair must be as flat as it will go. The top of the patient's head must be level with the top of the headrest.

The characteristics of perfect posture for the dentist should be:

1.  The long axis of the dentist's torso almost vertical with the shoulder line horizontal.

2.  The upper arms should hang vertically with the elbows in light contact with the ribcage.

    The importance of maintaining this contact cannot be emphasized enough. It is the key to working in perfect posture.

    There is an added and important advantage. The elbow contact will give a stabilizing point for the forearm and therefore the hands and fingers. This stabilisation in turn produces maximum control of the fingers and greater accuracy. The consequence is a higher quality of work by the dentist.

3.  The forearms are raised pivoting at the elbow joint to place the working point at the dentist's mid-sternal level. This will be explained later.

4.  The thighs splayed no more than 30 degrees apart with the hip line horizontal.

5.  The inter-pupillary line is horizontal.

6.  The dentist's head is tilted a maximum of 30 degrees to the horizontal.

7.  The dentist must sit so that he/she is as close to the top of the patient's head as possible. This prevents bending over to observe the work.

## Patient Height

The height of the patient's chair should be adjusted so that the working point in the patient's mouth is at the dentist's close focal distance - this is usually at mid-sternal or heart level and in the mid-line. With the patient in this position the dentist's forearms will slope upwards from elbows to fingertips. If they do it shows that the patient is at the correct height for the dentist.

Too many teachers maintain that the patient's head should be in or near the dentist's lap, but this is totally wrong. It places the working point beyond his focal distance and so causes the dentist to bend over in order to focus.

## Dental Stool

The dentist's stool should be adjusted in height so that when the dentist is seated the <u>upper</u> border of the thighs is at a minimum of 15 degrees to the horizontal. The stool itself should have a broad, rectangular (not round) seat to give plenty of support and it should also have a very firm and positive lumber support.

One of the few stools meeting these criteria is the Vinylmaster MDP.

Now that the dentist is correctly seated it is essential that the frontal plane of his/her face is parallel to the tooth surface being worked on. To maintain this it is helpful to employ the following Five Variables:

1. Move around the chair on your mobile stool between 0930 and 1230 positions. Never move past 0930 as the patient's shoulder will cause you to raise your elbow over it and so cause severe twisting of the upper body and neck.

   Moving past 1230 will impinge on the nurse's area and prevent her working with proper access and vision.

2. Rotate the patient's head left and right by up to 45 degrees to the vertical. This is well within the patient's comfort zone and you should never be afraid to rotate the patient's head to the full 45 degrees. It will be well tolerated by the patient.

3. Tilt the patient's head forward or backwards using the headrest itself or ask the patient to raise or lower their chin. One should always tilt the head forwards when working on lower teeth and backwards by up to 20 degrees below the horizontal if working on upper teeth. This is particularly important when using mirror vision.

4. Slightly close the patient's mouth when it is necessary. This relaxes the muscles and allows better access and vision to the working point.

5. The entire patient's chair should be raised or lowered so that the working point is at the correct mid-sternal height i.e. at the close focal distance of the operator.

There is one other factor which is vital to help maintain perfect posture. That is the utilization of a full-time chair side dental nurse – popularly known as four-handed dentistry or close support dentistry.

The nurse must be seated adjacent to the patient's shoulder with her left hip level with it and as close as possible.

Her eye level must be four inches higher than that of the dentist. This means she must work on a stool of the same design as the dentist but on a higher frame which places the seat higher. She must also have a footrest to enable her to sit comfortably, well-balanced and stable. Many dental nurses sit far too low and are unable to assist to the optimum efficiency. This is because nurses' stools, in general, do not go high enough. An ideal nurse's stool is the Vinylmaster MDPN.

The duties of a good dental nurse should be:-

- To prepare and organize the treatment area.
- Seat the patient correctly.
- Assist with the control of soft tissues and maintain access for the dentist.

- Maintain clear vision and access to the operating point by correctly using the aspirator and 3-in-1 syringe.
- Pass and exchange hand instruments and prepare and hand over necessary materials.

I cannot emphasise enough how much the dentist's quality of work and indeed quality of life can be improved by the correct employment of a good chair side nurse.

Finally it is essential to realize that dentistry is a static profession and that aerobic exercises should be performed on a regular basis by every dentist.

## Dr. Ellis Paul BDS, LDS, FFGDP RCS Eng, FICD

For full information on the course by Ellis and Jennifer Paul "Seated four-handed Dentistry" see www.seatedfourhandeddentistry.co.uk

For fuller information on this article please see the CD Rom "Perfect Posture for the Dental Team" by Ellis Paul obtainable from Smileon.com Treasure house, 19-21 Hatton Garden, London EC1N 8BA

For further information and questions please contact Ellis Paul on ellispauluk@gmail.com or telephone 0208 958 6547

The MDP and MDPN stools can be obtained from:
Jennifer Stanton, 50 Green Lane, Edgware, Middlesex HA8 7PX

# Raj Rattan -The KISS Principle

The word 'simplexity' when typed into word processing software generates a red, squiggly line beneath to indicate a misspelling. The word is not recognised in the software lexicon, but has been defined as *'the tendency of a simple system to generate complex forms.'* It is what has happened to the business of dentistry over recent years. Legislation, Regulation, and Clinical Guidelines are simple constructs, but generate convoluted forms by adding layers of complexity to what should be a simple, patient-centred business. The wave of simplexity brings the flotsam and jetsam we call uncertainty and fear - the mood-swingers of professionalism.

The wave speed and frequency in dentistry is unprecedented and increasing and in the words of the Roman poet Ovid, *'the cause is hidden; the effect is visible to all'* which, like ocean waves, emphasises the conspicuous nature of what is observable without necessarily citing the origin of the forces that give it momentum.

So, where does this analogy lead us and what does it mean? The challenge is one of managing the observed complexity. Consider the graph below; when rate of change (from c1 to c2) is slow paced, the time available to manage it is **t1**. When the complexity curve steepens as it does in times of rapid change, another doubling in complexity occurs, but the time available to manage is reduced to **t2**.

If this trend is extrapolated, the impact on dentistry is very significant because the time available to manage ever-increasing complexity is reduced on each occasion that the curve turns exponential leading to a point where we are drowned by the onslaught.

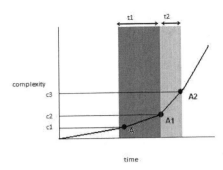

Legislative and regulatory imperatives have been the major drives of change in recent years, the 2006 contract, the publication of HTM01-05 and the requirements of registration with the Care Quality Commission (CQC) being just 3 examples.

Confusion, ambiguity, misinformation and, it must be said, disinformation help to create that complexity. Furthermore, whilst the intended consequences are explicit, it is the impact of the unintended consequences that compounds the perception of complexity. The old paradigm of *cause and effect* does not apply, partly of its latency (Ovid was right) and partly because of the unpredictability of unintended consequences – many of which are behavioural. Systems get blamed for behavioural change and professional values are sometimes eroded in the process. It is a phenomenon that adds another layer of complexity and one which Ann E. Tenbrunsel from the University of Notre Dame calls ethical fade. She posits that the 'should' self is replaced by the 'want' self, citing the misperception of individuals when it comes to either predicting their response to an ethical challenge or recalling a response from the past.

It is one of the challenges in the business of dentistry, identified by Ronald Wiebe, writing in the Journal of the Canadian Dental Association (The New Business Ethics 2000:66:248-249), where he states that *the private practitioner surviving on elective services is torn between the patient-first ethos of the healer and the survival-of-the-fittest demands of private enterprise.'*

Taken together, the pace of change, the lack of time to manage it effectively, the legislative and regulatory requirements inter-laced with ethical guidance and business challenges create a whirlpool of complexity that threatens our resilience on a daily basis, an attribute we cannot afford to lose.

So what actions do we need to take to improving our working lives? Put simply, we need to first remember the nature of our business. It is built on the purchase of credence not the purchase of dentistry; the latter is just the vehicle or carrier. In his book, **Reorganize for Resilience: Putting Customers at the Center of Your Organization** (January, 2010, Harvard Business Press), Professor Ranjay Gulati describes resilient businesses as those that prosper both in good times and bad; their growth and profitability driven by immersion in the lives of their customers. A patient-centred practice built of relationships will deliver this immersion. In my experience, a practice where *people buy people* is more resilient to the vicissitudes of the marketplace than a practice where patients buy dentistry.

Secondly, we must revert to the KISS principle: *keep it simple and straightforward* (or, *keep it simple stupid*, depending on your preferred reference for the acronym) and try and banish unnecessary complexity from dominating our working lives.

## Understanding Complexity

Let's look at three types of complexity.

- Apparent complexity
- Detail complexity
- Dynamic complexity

The first is illusory; there are simple patterns that lie beneath the surface. To discover the simple patterns, invest time to look for the root causes. It will be time well spent and will save anxiety and frustration at a later date.

Detail and dynamic complexity was described by Peter Senge in his book, The Fifth Discipline, where he writes that *'the real leverage in most management situations lies in understanding dynamic complexity not detail.'* What does this mean? It means that the real leverage in the management of a dental practice lies in understanding cause and effect and, importantly, the variations that can arise from that relationship. If you can manage the variation, you can control quality and run a better business. It comes from direct experience; from what Senge calls our *learning horizon*; there is no short-cut. Learn from every opportunity. It is what the Greeks called *praxis*.

Dynamic complexity arises when the cause and effect relationship is subtle and perhaps not immediately obvious and goes onto say that it occurs *'when the same action has dramatically different effects in the short run and the long, there is dynamic complexity. When an action has one set of consequences locally and a very different set of consequences in another part of the system, there is dynamic complexity.'* In contrast, detail complexity exists when there are many variables. When someone describes 25 techniques for preparing root canals for obturation, we are talking about detail complexity.

The world of dentistry is a world of dynamic complexity, both from a clinical and managerial standpoint. To improve our working lives, we must understand the linkages that drive our business, many of which are outlined in the concept of the Service-Profit Chain. It is the work of a group of researchers from Harvard; James L. Heskett, Thomas Jones, Gary Loveman, W. Earl Sasser, and Leonard Schlesinger some of whom later went on to write a book of the same name. The reader is referred to this text as an excellent reference source that describes the linkages which establish relationships between profitability, customer loyalty, and employee satisfaction, loyalty, and productivity.

In a clinical scenario, a typical example would be the treatment for a patient where the restorative work is dependent on the outcome of the periodontal status or an endodontic intervention which in turn may be related to an underlying periodontal defect. The diverse elements and variables for each specialist reflect detail complexity, whereas the number of interconnections and feedback loops over a period of time are examples of dynamic complexity.

Some of the common methods for managing complexity include:

- *Focus* – the vital few and the trivial many (see below)

- *Standardisation* – of systems and processes. For example, in order to meet CQC outcomes, a structured approach to creating a portfolio of evidence by standardising the format for each outcome simplifies the process and removes much of the perceived complexity of process. Add to it a simple system of management and what appears to be unbearable complexity is simplified.

- *Simple systems* – turning on a light switch is a simple task and produces a predictable outcome. It is the simplest of devices - a binary system: on/off. Simple systems are characterised by their reliability, predictability and their ability to be building blocks which can be stacked to manage complexity. Computers are complex, but reliant on the simplest construct - binary code. Using spread sheets as a business analysis tools simplifies the financial management of a practice, but it hides complicated algorithms and relationships. It shows that the complicated can be made less complex by simple, but scalable or stackable, systems.

- *Shared goals* – try and ensure that your team works to values rather than rules. This will help to reduce the behavioural variances which are unsettling. Shared goals also create synergy and empower the team in a business and will create outputs (as measured by various metrics) greater than the sum of the individual parts. The added value created through this limits dynamic complexity and makes inherent complexity easier to manage.

# The vital few and the trivial many

Learning to make the best use of (less and less) time is an essential skill to master complexity because it distils the vital elements from the trivial. Known as *The Pareto Principle*, it was first described by the 19th Century Italian economist, Vilfredo Pareto, who formulated what he called "*The Law of the Unequal Distribution'* (after observing the distribution of wealth amongst Italian citizens). It is commonly known as the *80/20 rule;* Pareto had noted that 80% of Italy's wealth was held by 20% of its citizens.

It was George Zipf, a Harvard professor of philosophy, who popularised the concept by calling it the *Principle of Least Effort* citing that typically 20% of a resource (human or otherwise) accounted for 70-80 per cent of the activity related to that resource. The leverage will help to simplify management activities and reduce complexity. For example,

- In commercial terms, 20 % of a company's products/services may account for 80% of its profits.
- In the case of computer software, 20 % of the features are used 80% of the time.
- In restaurants, 80% of the meals come from 20% of the menu

If 20% of a person's effort generates 80% of the results then the corollary is that 20% of the results we achieve take up some 80% of our effort. The challenge in the management of complexity is to identify the vital 20% elements that contribute to the complexity and focus on those and not be distracted by the 'trivial' 80%.

Consider these observations as a starting point. They have been gathered from personal observations made over the years:

- 80% of the key decisions in meetings arise from only 20% of the meeting time.
- 80% of your practice management time is spent on 20% of tasks
- 80% of complaints are about the same 20% of services
- 80% of absences arise from the same 20% of your team

- 80% of your success comes from 20% of your efforts
- 80% of your equipment repair bill will be generated by 20% of your equipment

The value of this observation to any individual or organisation determined to achieve more is to note that if you could double your top 20 % of activities, you could work a 2-day week and achieve 60 per cent more.

## Ockham's razor

What this chapter has been about is a very old principle known as Ockham's razor.

It was the 14th century theologian and Franciscan friar, William of Ockham who stated '*Entia non sunt multiplicanda praeter necessitatem*' which translates to *entities must not be multiplied beyond what is necessary*. It is also known as the Principle of Parsimony. In other words, if you have two equally likely solutions to a problem, choose the simplest; it is often the most effective. It is a principle that applies as much to practice management as it does to clinical practice, the trend towards minimally invasive dentistry being a prime example of the razor at work and brings us back to the title of this chapter.

It is referred to as a 'razor' because it shaves off the extraneous and the unnecessary leaving behind only the essential and has been cited by the world's greatest thinkers. Stephen Hawking in his book *A Brief History of Time* writes "*We could still imagine that there is a set of laws that determines events completely for some supernatural being, who could observe the present state of the universe without disturbing it. However, such models of the universe are not of much interest to us mortals. It seems better to employ the principle known as Ockham's razor and cut out all the features of the theory that cannot be observed.*"

.

# Summary

Complexity arises from diversity, inter-dependence, and ambiguity. To be effective in the clinical care of our patients and resilient in our businesses, we must unravel unnecessary complexity. In the words of Albert Einstein, *everything should be made as simple as possible, but not simpler.* Take too much out with the razor and you will affect function and purpose; shave away just the right amount and we can improve our working lives.

**Raj Rattan MBE, BDS, MFGDP, FFGDP Dip.MDE**

# Alun Rees - The science of finding, building and keeping the perfect team.

"None of us is as good as all of us" Sir John Hegarty

The main problems faced by Dental Practice owners fall into one of three groups:

- **Time.**
- **People.**
- **Money.**

My experience has shown that, whilst time and money are very important, it is impossible to build a truly successful dental business unless you get the people right. All principals face the challenge of recruiting, training and retaining a great team whether they are running a one dentist set up or a chain of practices. It is estimated that, across the board, close to 50% of staff recruited stay in post for fewer than 12 months. The cost in cash, time and team morale is immeasurable. Yet most practices keep on doing what they have always done and hope that they will get different results. My emails regularly bring me stories of:

- **Team members recruited who turn out to be not quite what they seemed.**
- **Problems with practices retaining staff.**
- **Difficulties integrating the individuals into a team.**
- **Hygienists & Therapists being "outside the wire".**
- **Associates failing to embrace the practice vision.**

In order to achieve "best practice" dentists are encouraged to work using evidence based dentistry. They ought also, as business owners, look beyond their immediate sphere and learn from other professions and industries. There is an established system that has been proven to work in many hundreds of businesses around the world with hundreds of thousands of individual results.
It's called Kolbe Wisdom™ and it:

- **Identifies the striving instincts that drive natural behaviours.**
- **Focuses on the strengths of your team.**

The KOLBE A Index is a 36-question survey that reveals the individual mix of striving instincts; it measures individual energies in four Action Modes:

- **Fact Finder** – Gathering and sharing of information.
- **Follow through** – Sorting and Storing Information.
- **Quick Start** – Dealing with risk and uncertainty.
- **Implementation** – Handling space and intangibles.

Each Action Mode has three Zones of Operation, which determine how the individual acts when using it.

- **Initiating Zone**: how they insist on beginning the problem-solving process. (7-10)
- **Accommodation Zone**: how they respond to people and situations. (4-6)
- **Preventing Zone:** how they avoid or resist problems. (0-3)

The results are a serious of 'scores'. Mine for instance is 6:3:8:3, this isn't the place to give full analysis, my partner's is 8:8:1:4 the main result is that we complement each other, perhaps that's the reason that we have worked together successfully for 30 years. The Kolbe Wisdom™ is based on the concept that creative instincts are the source of the mental energy that drives people to take specific actions. This mental drive is separate and distinct from passive feelings and thoughts. Creative instincts are manifested in an innate pattern (*modus operandi*, or MO) that determines each person's best efforts. Conation doesn't define what you can or can't do, rather what you will and won't do.

Someone's MO is quantifiable and observable; yet functions at the subconscious level. MOs vary across the general population with no gender, age or racial bias. An individual's MO governs actions, reactions and interactions. It also determines a person's use of time and his or her natural form of communication. Exercising control over this mental resource gives people the freedom to be their authentic selves. Any interference with the use of this energy reduces a person's effectiveness and the joy of accomplishment. Stress inevitably results from the prolonged disruption of the flow of this energy. Others can nurture this natural ability but block it by attempting to alter it.

Individual performance can be predicted with great accuracy by comparing instinctive realities, self-expectations and requirements. It will fluctuate based on the appropriateness of expectations and requirements. When groups of people with the right mix of MOs function interactively, the combined mental energy produces synergy. Such a team can perform at a higher level than is possible for the same group functioning independently.

The mind has three basic features:
- **Cognitive** relates to knowledge or intelligence. It tells you what you can or can't do and is measured by IQ, and similar, tests.
- **Affective** relates to attitudes, beliefs or values. It tells you what you want to do and can be measured by MBTI, DISC and several other systems.
- **Conative** relates to instinct or natural energy and is measured by use of the **Kolbe Index.**

The Kolbe Index has been shown to be consistent over periods of many years. As a potential employer or someone looking to build a team that you can predict and rely upon for consistency this is most important. The measures of the Affective mentioned earlier can change dramatically in a relatively short space of time, MBTI as much as 50% in six weeks, which is clearly unacceptable. Kolbe is a straightforward, simple to remember, system that tells you how employees and colleagues approach their work and problem solving, and how they will **act** during stressful times. Let's face it that's really what we want to know when we hire someone or work with them on a team isn't it?

# Let's look at Kolbe at work.
## Case Study 1

Jimmy and Kate run a one-dentist dental practice, which they bought as a run-down practice. They have successfully converted it from a large dependence on the NHS to 100% private.

|        | Fact Finder | Follow Through | Quick Start | Implementation |
|--------|-------------|----------------|-------------|----------------|
| Jimmy  | 4           | 5              | 3           | 8              |
| Kate   | 5           | 3              | 8           | 5              |
| Susanna| 7           | 6              | 4           | 3              |
| Marion | 7           | 8              | 2           | 3              |

Jimmy (4:5:3:8) is a dentist who is technically excellent and loves nothing more than expanding his clinical knowledge. Kate's (5:3:8:5) background is in dental nursing, in the past she has worked for a small corporate in a management position; she admits that her real love is working with people. They have a full-time receptionist, Susanna, (7:6:4:3), a hygienist Marion (5:7:3:5) and a dental nurse, Jane, (7:8:2:3).

Kate has been trying to act as a practice manager and, whilst she can cope with the systems desperately misses regular contact with patients, but feels guilty about "not pulling her weight" in the office.

What do their MO's tell us? Jimmy's "8" in Implementor means that he is well suited to working with his hands, he will prevent stress by acting skilfully, mechanically and dexterously. His "3" in Quick Start means that he *prevents* in that mode, his instinct wants to keep things on track, he dislikes working to deadlines and tends towards the status quo. If change is inevitable he wants to understand how and why and he will then prevent chaos.

Kate's "8" means that she initiates in Quick Start, her "3" means that she resists in "Follow Through". Her instinct means that she thrives on short deadlines, loves the flexibility of having several balls in the air at once, she's an improviser. She's far more of a natural entrepreneur than her husband and business partner, which resulted in stresses between them until they understood their "Kolbes".

Susanna scores highest in "Fact Finder" and is well suited for a post of receptionist, she asks lots of questions and is good on long term projects although she needs to be reminded of deadlines as there may be a tendency to keep researching. Her "3" in Implementor means that she imagines ideas or concepts without the physical structure. The real light bulb moment came when Jimmy and Kate realised not only why she (Kate) was struggling with the Practice Manager role but also that she was the ideal person to fulfil the role of treatment co-ordinator that none of the rest of the team suited. Also Jimmy was able to come to terms with his misgivings about expanding the practice.

They decided to recruit a practice manager and to help them with this I was able to produce a synergy chart showing where they were lacking energy, what different individuals might offer and how they would fit.

|       | Fact Finder | Follow Through | Quick Start | Implementation |
|-------|-------------|----------------|-------------|----------------|
| Dawn  | 5           | 6              | 3           | 6              |
| Emily | 7           | 4              | 6           | 3              |

Two individuals were short-listed for the post, Dawn (MO 5:6:3:6) and Emily (7:4:6:3). Differences between them were in "Quick Start" Dawn was a "stabiliser", Emily a "modifier" and in "Implementor" Dawn was a "restorer" and Emily an "imaginer". Of significance was where their MOs fitted into the synergy chart of Natural Talents that I had produced. My advice was to give the job to Dawn but they had been more impressed with Emily in the interview, she was offered the post and accepted.

Two weeks after she started work I called them to see how everything was going, "a complete disaster" was how it was put to me. All my misgivings were correct, she showed no signs of being able to work with the rest of the team or on her own, tasks started were never finished and there was a tendency to ignore or just not accept deadlines.

Thankfully, Dawn was still in the market and accepted the post, two years on she's still in post and is a valuable member of the team. Her tendency to stabilise is still there but Kate and Jimmy can work with that and know what to look for when they are working with her. More to the point they still give thanks for the fact they were able to see why Emily was wrong for the post, it wasn't just a new employee settling in it was a matter of synergy. It might have taken months or years to realise what was wrong and they would have then possibly be faced with the challenges of employment law.

## Case Study 2

Mike and Neil are two practice owners. For several years they have been running their own successful "one-man bands" with varying amounts of staff support. Occasionally Neil provides holiday cover for Mike and has taken some referrals from him for the specific skills that he has developed. They each have support teams; Mike has a part-time but enthusiastic associate, Oliver and works with his partner, Philippa, who is a hygienist.

|                     | Fact Finder | Follow Through | Quick Start | Implementor |
|---------------------|-------------|----------------|-------------|-------------|
| Michael- Principal  | 5           | 5              | 7           | 3           |
| Neil - Principal    | 4           | 5              | 8           | 4           |
| Oliver - Associate  | 6           | 3              | 8           | 3           |
| Philippa- Hyg       | 7           | 3              | 6           | 3           |
| Rosie - Recep/PM    | 7           | 8              | 3           | 2           |

After several months of discussion and enthusiasm they decide to go into partnership together. They will be expense-sharing partners, the business is launched and almost immediately there are operative problems. Both partners are enthusiastic about using Kolbe in recruitment but make the fundamental error of failing to look at themselves as part of the bigger picture, in fact one of them says "this is bound to be a success we're practically Kolbe twins."

That optimistic statement is one of the keys to their failure. Both Michael & Neil Initiate in Quick Start, Respond in Follow Through & Fact Finder and have very similar scores for Implementor where they tend to Prevent.

Oliver also initiates in Quick Start so you have 3 individuals who will:

- **Take risks**
- **Create a sense of urgency**
- **Initiate change**
- **Seek Challenges**
- **Create Innovation**
- **Act on Intuition**

Now these characteristics are great for individual entrepreneurs but they need to be balanced by one or more people within the organisation who can Initiate in Follow Through & Implementor.

Rosie & Philippa who score highly in Fact Finder end up researching and researching until they come close to "Perfection Paralysis", Rosie is the only person who initiates in Follow Through and she becomes overwhelmed.

The organisation lacked anyone who initiates in Implementor, there is no one who:

- **Has a Time Zone that is the Present**
- **Is grounded in the here and now, who can create quality products that will endure through time.**
- **Communicates using props, models & demonstrations.**
- **Stores Information by Quality**
- **Works with models or prototypes**
- **Requires concrete, demonstrable goals that have lasting value.**

So, the partners, always looking at the future, dominated business meetings, the practice manager trying to provide the information gets bogged down in detail.

What the leadership needed was someone who Initiated or Responded in Implementor and either Prevented or Responded in Quick Start, which would have brought the Team Synergy back to the appropriate levels. Unfortunately although those individuals might well have been available the partners' "rush" was not balanced sufficiently from the outset and failure was inevitable.

The venture lasted as a going concern for fewer than nine months and the episode soured the personal relationships of most of those involved. The two main protagonists have gone back to being – in the main – their own **"bosses"**.

Experience shows that there is more to recruitment and team building than advertising and trusting to CVs and interviews. Kolbe certificated consultants are few and far between outside the USA but for those practices who want to take their team building to the level of their clinical skills an investment in their skills is a must.

## Alun Rees BDS

**www.alunrees.com**

Business coaching for professional people

# John Renshaw - Take Control of Your Life

When I started in practice in Scarborough back in 1969 I did what most others would have done in the circumstances. I fell in with the way the place was run, I turned up and dealt with the toothaches, I planned some simple treatment for patients and I picked up where my predecessor left off. He had been in practice for fifteen years and left to go to Zambia – maybe I should have read more into that particular feature of the story than I did!

I was fine, I was young, I was busy, and I was making enough to live on. I was finding my feet in a new town, finding a place to live and setting out my direction of travel – as far as the nearest pub, that is. I had no long term goals and no idea what the future might hold and very little real interest in it to be honest. I had spent too many years grafting and managing on little or no money to pass up the chance to enjoy having a good time with cash in my pocket.

After a few months the issue of a partnership came up (my predecessor had left without selling his share of the practice – don't ask). **Did I want to stay in Scarborough?** I had only thought originally about having a good time at the seaside for a few months. **Did I want to be a partner in a busy NHS / private mixed practice?** (The practice was doing about 20% private in 1969 – think about that. At the time the rest of dentistry was doing 94% NHS and 6% private).

I joined up for the princely sum of £1500. You might guess that I had already learned how to negotiate, the outgoing partner had little or nothing to sell having abandoned his partner and his share of the practice to undertake what turned out to be a fifteen year sojourn across Africa and the South Pacific with the Crown Agents – as they were known back then.

I took on the organisational role and learned how to run a practice the hard way (my business partner was then 58 years old, I was just 24). I didn't really have much of a clue, I had one or two local friends but no mentor (didn't know what one of those was) and no financial advice (accountants prepared the accounts about six months after the year end in those days).

The pressure was mounting – work, running the practice, juggling a life full of expensive new pastimes, buying a nice house, working more to fund the lifestyle, spending more, working ever harder to fund the expanding cost of the profligate lifestyle, acquiring substantial debts. At least I was lucky enough to have no student debt to pay off. My approach to the local Midland Bank Manager (a lifelong friend eventually) was to seek his support of my existing overdraft from Leeds – the gargantuan sum of £35. After five years at University that was the sum total of my debts. Yes, I do know how lucky I was.

My life was out of control. I somehow could never manage to earn enough to beat the bills. No matter what I did, the bills always came out on top in the month end fight for my cheque book (no credit cards in those days). I bought a second practice, I employed three associates. My older partner retired and I bought him out. I was a first class amateur golfer off a handicap of four or five for almost twenty years.

The number of patients I was seeing daily on the NHS was rising steadily. I had never been the most assiduous worker. I used to think 20 a day was a lot, and then it was 25, then 30, then 35 and eventually 40 or more. And that was on top of everything else I was doing.
After ten years in practice I finally stopped, looked around and asked myself one simple question –

**"What in God's name do you think you are doing?"**

I did not think I was doing exceptional treatment, I was not making bundles of cash, I did not feel particularly valued by my patients and my work / life balance was deteriorating rapidly. I just could not run fast enough. Something had to be done – but what? Who did I talk to? I didn't have anyone to turn to that I trusted. I felt isolated and abandoned but the person who was abandoned was me and the person doing the abandoning was also me. I did know that the fault lay with me and I realised that the answer lay with me as well.


### Lesson 1 emerges at this point of the story :
**Don't look to blame others for what you have done to yourself**

I thought about this for a long time because there were no 'Godfathers' out there to offer help in those days. Most people thought that the NHS was the answer to everyone's prayers and why would it ever change? I had very different views of the future. By this time I had developed a second career on the political wing of UK dentistry and the wider UK healthcare scene. I was climbing the dento-political greasy pole in Yorkshire and had set my first foot on the national scene as well.

I wanted to secure a better deal for the youngsters coming into the profession. I knew the dentistry game had treated me well but I also knew others who had not been so lucky. It dawned on me that I had two key problems facing me and I identified two key responses that would help to put things right.

### My first enemy was poor time management.

It took me years to recognise that I was simply a victim of the system that operated within the practice I owned. I had fallen in with the way of things from the very start and had made no real effort to improve my daily working life. I did a full day of clinical work and all the rest had to be fitted in somewhere in between. The stress levels were reaching the danger mark. My first marriage broke up – mostly my fault.


### Lesson 2 is perhaps more important than lesson 1 :
**Don't accept the *status quo* if you don't like it**

I moved on and soon learned lesson three. I was blessed with a vile temper and a bullying demeanour, a big man with a big voice and a big chip on his shoulder. If I wanted to change my life for the better I had to find a better method of communicating with other people or they just wouldn't listen to me - talk about facing up to the cold light of reality!

## Lesson 3  Understand the difference between assertiveness and aggression

Assertiveness is not shouting and bawling, throwing your toys out of the pram and being generally obnoxious. It's simply saying what you mean, meaning what you say and saying it quietly, again and again until people understand that you intend to do what you say, that you are consistent, reliable and fair.

I changed my appointment book with a lot of help from my head receptionist. It took almost two years to get it where I wanted it. I learned to say no to new patients – stopping the flood of new patients was the best thing I ever did – until I was ready to ease the flow back. I learned how to talk sensibly to potential private patients about the benefits of cosmetic dentistry in the mid 1980s – long before it was fashionable. I set a limit of 30 patients a day and told staff I intended to stick to it, come what may. I gradually reduced the number to 25 and when I finally left the NHS in 2006 I decided that

## "Twenty is Plenty"

Staff found me less inclined to fly off the handle. My new wife supported me consistently and helped me make sense out of my new developing life. I began to make reasonable money (profit has never been a fixation with me), my kids were going to public school and, eventually beyond that. My political career was taking off and I had good committee jobs with real responsibility – just what I wanted, an opportunity to input at a high level on the national healthcare policy scene.

The building blocks were simple. The effects were not dramatic to begin with, they took time to play out, about four or five years for the transformation to be complete. The result was a long career, I'm still doing four days' clinical work each week at the age of 65 and running a busy consultancy company (Oral Care Consulting Ltd – **www.oralcareconsulting.com**) offering much needed help and support to the kind of people I used to be – intelligent – yes, talented – yes, cash rich – yes, time poor – yes, able to forward plan – you must be joking! Knowing where they are heading – hardly.

Life is never easy and we all make mistakes. I have made more than my fair share. The trick is to not keep on making the same mistakes again and again, expecting by some inexplicable miracle that the result will somehow change.

We only get one go at this life and it is up to each of us to make of it what we will. Listening to others who have been there and seen what it is all about is not wasted time. What you hear may seem irrelevant but buried inside it is the essence of what's right and wrong, what generally works, what helps build a successful professional career and if you are really lucky – a good life.

# John Renshaw BChD, DGDP

## www.oralcareconsulting.com

John has been a general dental practitioner in Scarborough for 42 years (37 years in the NHS).

He was President of the Yorkshire Branch of the British Dental Association in 1983 and again in 2006 - the only person ever to hold that office twice. He was a member of two health authorities for 15 years and a Dental Practice Adviser for 12 years. He was Chairman of the BDA's Executive Board from 2000 to 2005. He was the only General Dental Practitioner ever to chair the Department of Health's Standing Dental Advisory Committee.

# Steve Van Russelt - Do you need a dental practice website?

As a practice owner or potential practice owner it will have occurred to you that you should consider having an 'online presence' to complement your business. Websites are increasingly an expected and integral part of a dental practice, in common with most other businesses. Perhaps you keep asking yourself why you haven't yet got around to it.

Having said that, a website isn't essential, but you would probably feel better if you could tick that tick-box in your head that keeps telling you that it is a good idea.

Websites come in many varieties so you have several options to consider, from the 'all-singing and dancing' interactive website, to a 'brochure' site, which is simply a page or two with contact details and condensed essential information. There is a place for these two types of site sitting at the extremes of the spectrum and all that lie in-between.

Let's look at what is available in the round, categorised into three groups;

## The bespoke site:

You may well have set aside a marketing budget for your dental practice; business coaches will tell you that you should. In that case a proportion may be lent to the task of website production, perhaps employing a company that will integrate a website with the branding of the practice. This might include logo production, the practice decoration, uniforms and stationery; all aimed at the image that you wish to present and the target audience that you serve or would wish to serve.

In this sector you can certainly spend your money and you make your choice, a bespoke site should be made from the ground up,

containing individualised graphics, custom photography, perhaps even including models pictured in your practice, and additionally might include the commissioning of a smartphone application. Without having to go to the lengths of having such an 'app' produced, some modern site templates can detect if the website is being accessed through a smartphone, and will then present information differently to better suit the small screen size.
Obviously there are many companies competing for your business in the UK and abroad- the internet is global after all. Several companies are available that specialise in producing sites for dental practices only. If this is what you are looking for, in the same way that we gain our own patients, look for recommendations, check out the web designers' portfolios, choose people that you get along with and who have a proven track record. The main players are usually to be found at dental exhibitions where you will have the opportunity to question them directly. Be prepared to have to pay them a significant amount for a fully bespoke site.

## The templated site aimed at dental practices:

Several companies have established models that give customers the facility to produce a website by typing in their own content online, add a few photographs and choose from one of the available preset templates, which will give the site its look. They may also offer generic patient guides, but that sort of information is readily available from other sites on the internet and adds little value.
Be conscious of the fact that like a *Yellow Pages* advert, without your input such a site could then remain static for years, with relatively high costs for the end result. The term 'money for old rope' comes to mind. Nowadays you can readily produce your own site which would at least match and hopefully exceed the quality of such a site at a much lower cost.

## The DIY site:

Many a dentist has in the past taken a copy of *Microsoft Publisher*© and used it to produce a rudimentary website subsequently uploaded to some free web space. Unfortunately a lot of these are still out there and quite frankly are counter-productive; they would be better not existing at all.

Today though with software that can be acquired at no cost, you can, should you wish, produce with some of your spare time a high quality website that would be indistinguishable to many a commercially produced site, with the ability to easily make any changes to it in future with no further costs involved. Given the modern software tools that have become available, if you are familiar with a personal computer and the programs that are now commonly used from day to day, you should be able to produce such a site without a great deal of expense, using either local or online software. This functionality was not the case until relatively recently, and can give you the satisfaction of producing your own site. Perhaps you enjoy photography and the whole digital 'thing', then you could happily apply yourself to such a project. There are several ways of achieving this:

- **Content Management Systems (CMS).** Most of these work with a collection of files on the server, with the content and settings of the site stored in an online database. There are many different packages, and most of them are free to download and use. Two which stand out are *Joomla!* and *Wordpress.* There are a multitude of different templates available, be it free or at low cost to alter the appearance of the site. If you are unfamiliar with setting such a site up, some webhosts provide 'one-click' set-up which installs the software for you. Editing of the content is accomplished with online editors, enabling you to add text and upload graphics. This is not though an out-of-the box solution for those that have no previous experience of producing such a site, practice is required.
- **Online Website Builders.** Most mainstream web hosting companies along with those that just specialise in this sector provide software that you can use online to create a site, again fitting your content into a template of your choosing. Just carry out a web search for 'Website Builder, and you will see that you are spoilt for choice. Some of the sites

produced look better than others dependant on the software used and the number of templates available, take your time and have a look at the sample sites produced by several packages if you are thinking of taking this route. Take a look at *moonfruit.com* as an example.

- **Local Software**. Traditionally sites were built from scratch using *Frontpage©* or *Dreamweaver©* on your own computer and then uploaded to the internet. This sort of software is not very user-friendly for those new to website design, being more of a professional tool. The number of more user-friendly software packages has expanded where you edit the site on your computer before uploading the files to the internet via a process called File Transfer Protocol (FTP). These are usually low cost or free.

## Domain names:

Make sure that you acquire a good domain name and that you have ownership and control of it. Try and make sure that is not overly long, *mainroadspecialistdentalpracticeandspa.co.uk* might describe your practice but it doesn't trip off the tongue. Secure your investment and repel the cyber squatters by purchasing hyphenated versions of the key domain name. If you were to acquire for example mypractice.co.uk, you might also look to purchase my-practice.co.uk as well as the two .com versions. All of these can be made to point to the same website, but focus on one as the address that you give out. The traditional suffixes are really quite cheap these days, and like a cherished car registration plate, once somebody else has purchased the domain name that you want to own, then it is gone. It's at that point that you really wish that you had bought them. Don't take this to extremes, there are so many suffixes available now to purchase, but you may want to consider including the recently introduced .co suffix as well. Use email addresses that employ your domain name rather than for example, hotmail addresses.

## Site Content:

We have busy working lives and would like our websites to look after themselves, but they do need maintaining. A jaded out-of-date site will give patients the wrong impression. Ask the question about the costs of upgrading your site and adding new content if it is not editable by you. Ideally you should be able to edit the site yourself, or have an agreed number of modifications per year included in the ongoing cost.

One way of keeping the content fresh is to install an application that can take Tweets or Facebook messages and incorporate them into the page. Social media has become all pervasive and accounts for a considerable percentage of internet traffic.

Patient testimonials are a valuable addition, and increasingly video testimonials are being employed.

A few things to avoid:
- An introductory flash movie (that everybody skips).
- Scrolling marquees
- Narrow pages – screen resolutions have come on since the 800 pixel screen.
- Words underlined or emboldened under the misapprehension that this will help with Search Engine Optimisation (SEO).
- A musical background or flash graphic that restarts every time a new page is opened.
- Lashings of Stock photographs of people that are obviously Americans!

A few essentials:
- Follow the regulatory guidelines stated below
- Make sure your site is backed up after changes are made so that it can be easily restored should problems occur – for example web server hard drives can fail like any other
- Consider changing the site's appearance occasionally to keep it novel – this can be easily achieved with templated sites.
- Keep it updated!

## Google, search engines and SEO.

Google should be your friend; they are potentially a very powerful force to help you market your site. They can also provide you with detailed information about the visitors to your site through their freely available 'Webmaster Tools'.

Many companies offer to optimise your site with the aim of pushing your listing up to the top of the search engine results pages, to the extent that emails promoting this service have become a form of spam. Obviously not everybody can be at the top and I am not sure that this can give a good return on investment, but there are a few things that you can do yourself to improve your ranking:

- Consider spending some of your marketing budget on Adwords – Google's advertising system that produces sponsored adverts. Look out for free Google Adsense vouchers in magazines; you can test the water without any initial cost. Advertising in this manner appears to make the omnipotent Google look on you in a good light and consequently improves your website rankings
- Generate a sitemap that Google can crawl more easily to add your pages to its database
- Add 'alt' and 'title' tags to all of your images with a short description of the content of the image
- Get other sites to link to you – the more the merrier
- Get listed at dmoz.org, a lot of other search engines grab their data from that site
- Use free software to submit your site to many search engines at once

## Regulatory body requirements for websites:

Dental practices have become the most regulated of all professions, and as you would expect, regulation extends to dental practice websites, increasingly from the General Dental Council and also under the umbrella of the *Council of European Dentists,* which produces the EU Manual of Dental Practice.

Thankfully the requirements are not overly-burdensome. The regulations include guidance on the choice of domain names, also the required and discretionary information to be made available on the website.

You can find the current guidance by following this internet link: **http://tinyurl.com/EUdental** . You should also consider any data protection implications and ensure that your site is secure especially if you are storing visitor login details for member-restricted parts of the site.

# Steve Van Russelt BDS

A general dental practitioner with an interest in website production, he has produced a number of sites for dental organisations and provides technical support for the GDPUK.com website.

**info@theDental.biz**

# Sheila Scott - Paying attention to trust, health and sterilisation

I've been working with dentists and their teams for over 20 years now, and I'd say that the most useful thing I've ever asked my clients to do is a little in depth patient research. Before making any plans for strategic changes, or improvements to patient care routines, I've always talked to the practice's patients, observed routine patient contacts, conducted focus group sessions, talked to teams and so on. But what's taught me and the practices most has been collecting quantitative and qualitative information about what's most important to patients and what they think of the patient service so far.

At the time of writing, many dentists feel pushed into doing patient questionnaires in order to satisfy new requirements. But the real reasons for doing patient questionnaires is to help the practice make good decisions about the service provided and how communications should be structured; to help the practice become a better one.

- **This is evidence based practice development.**
- **It means that the practice knows exactly how it can improve patients' satisfaction with the service provided.**
- **It means that the practice knows exactly what it can do to make or keep patients happy.**
- **And that makes a huge difference to patients, the team, the practice fortunes – and usually, to the happiness of the practice owner.**

The most important thing my questionnaires have shown over the years is that patients' priorities when visiting, using and judging their practices are completely at odds with those that dentists and teams choose on behalf of their patients.

Teams believe that concepts such as 'gentleness', 'good pain control', 'convenient appointment times' and 'low costs' are vital to attracting and keeping good patients. They believe that patients increasingly want 'cosmetic treatments' and fill their waiting rooms full of whitening posters, and their websites of pictures of cosmetic enhancements.

Whilst all of these aspects are very important to selective patients, a definite priority becomes clear when a population of patients is asked to rate a number of concepts. Dentists and teams are shocked, when they find that three of the above concepts only make the bottom of patients' lists.

For years, the number one priority for patients when choosing and using a dental practice has been 'trust', followed closely by 'treatments to ensure teeth and gums stay healthy' and 'sterilisation/patient protection'. There are other concepts that consistently score at the top of the list when patients rate what's important to them, and there are some differences between practices in rank orders. But these three concepts are definitely top priority in dental practices in the UK and Ireland

So in order to better satisfy patients and make practice success and happiness easier to achieve, practices must organise to deliver these without fail.

## Trust

How to deliver trust? This is a difficult concept to define exactly, and the research on this aspect is quite sparse, but we all know instinctively when *we* trust a professional, and more specifically when we don't. This is a great topic for regular team debate at practice meetings, and there are a variety of techniques to be used to help the team come up with recommendations and action plans. Some of my favourite of these include:

1. **Discussion**: What makes us lose trust in other providers – could we be allowing our patients to react in the same way? It's interesting how passionate we get when talking about providers that have let us down! Let the energy in the descriptions of poor service be a warning to all – and make

sure your practice adopts routines to prevent any hint of a similar reaction!

2. **Discussion/training**: Do we need to agree communications routines, to include attention to the many non-verbal clues that patients can interpret as showing interest – or none – when interacting?

3. **Team game**: Swop roles for 20 minutes. In teams, nurses pretend they're dentists; dentists -hygienists; hygienists-receptionists etc. Now, in the new teams, complete the sentence in at least three ways... '**If I were a (new role), and I wanted patients to really trust me and what I do, I'd...................**' This is a fun and non threatening way to suggest improvements in how the team work with patients, and we usually open up debate on very pertinent and important issues.

## Health

My research has told me that 'keeping me healthy' is a vital priority for patients. It is also a vital aim of the service of most practices. Yet it is an area where most practices miss opportunities to impress, instead focusing - promotionally - on cosmetic dentistry, and in everyday routines - on finding problems to fix in mouths.

Much of my work with practices is about helping to refocus care and routines to prove that attention to dental health is paramount. In a fully preventive (health focused) approach, we also find that restorative and cosmetic options are more easily – and happily – accepted.

The classic opening line in the regular exam for example, subtly communicates focus. Is your first question of patients 'Any problems?' (subtext; you're looking for a problem to fix), or 'How healthy do you feel your teeth and gums are just now?' (subtext; you're hoping to give me what I'm hoping for – a clean bill of health!)

I ask my practices to let their patients know they are 'healthy' in as many aspects of dental health as possible – not waiting until the end of a full examination where up to 16 different aspects of health have been assessed and just saying the patient is 'fine'. Instead, health focused practitioners tell patients that their teeth are 'strong and healthy' (or not); that their restorations are 'stable and healthy' (or not); their gums are 'healthy' (or not); that the inside of their mouth is 'healthy' (and by the way, that was your Oral Cancer Check' – another priority for patients that is much more important than dentists and teams suspect); their bite seems 'healthy'(or not) etc etc.

This needn't take an extra ten minutes either – most of my practices provide a quick ticked paper/printed summary of the well- defined and full 12/14/16 point Dental Health Check.- so much more than 'just' a 'check up'. I believe that it's vital that practices prove to patients that the most important appointment they ever provide, is much more than the default belief that the dental exam is a 30 second look in the mouth for 'holes'.

Most practices can also make their referrals to hygienists much more effective – by adding a sentence or two about what the purpose of the hygiene appointment is and why regular hygiene appointment are important and essential. The secret to keeping a hygiene book full, has so much more to do with effective communications from dentists than it has to do with missed appointment charges!

## Sterilisation

The practise of cross infection control becomes more meticulous every year, and vast sums of money are spent on decontamination rooms and equipment. But as the processes have been moved from the autoclave in the corner of the surgery to areas tucked away out of sight, patients' confidence in their safety in the practices has dropped dramatically. Routines may be 99% perfect, but it's essential also that patents *perceive* the same! It's time to take those sterilisation routines out of the closet and prove the practice's attention...

If possible, decontamination or sterilisation rooms should be visible to patients. I love glass fronted areas that have huge letters spelling out 'Sterilisation' etched across them. Or signage indicating where the sterilisation room is.

Teams need to be seen to following good cross infection routines – obvious hand washing/hand rubbing, surface disinfecting, disposing of disposables, holding of gloved hands high, so as to appear to avoid contamination, etc, can make a huge difference to patient perceptions. Clinical teams should use the word 'sterile' at least once in every patient appointment (**'Can I have a sterile xxy?'** **'Here's your sterile tray'**, **'I'll just get a sterile yyx'** etc.). Sterilisation co-ordinators need to make sure they are noticed/ heard when they pop in for the 'tray for sterilising' or they 'take this to the decontamination room'.

Absolute cleanliness, clear surfaces, and much *shine* also seem to help enormously in this area – and conversely, the absence of any of these reduces patient confidence.

Almost every practice can improve its performance in each of the three areas above, to help impress patients, build their loyalty, appreciation, and likelihood to refer more friends and family. But it is also important that each practice investigates its own patients' priorities and perceptions of each aspect. And then, of course, each practice has to take action on the findings to work towards a more successful practice and a better working life!

## Sheila Scott

**www.sheila-scott.co.uk**

Sheila has been a business consultant to dentists and dental practices for over 20 years, and has built up a massive knowledge about what makes a dental practice successful and profitable.

# Joe Sullivan - A Creative Illness. From Stress to Success

It is said that dentistry is a stressful profession. Surprisingly, although we perform complicated procedures on people who feel vulnerable, frightened and are perhaps highly stressed, many dentists enjoy their work. For some however it is stressful all of the time. It is seldom the job in itself that is stressful. There are those who specialise in the various fields of our profession, performing procedures all day which are extreme stressors for others. As I approach the final part of my practising life I am enjoying dentistry very much and have done for years. But in terms of stress it was not always so.

A few years ago I gave a talk to a group of Vocational Trainee dentists. My topic was stress and stress management. The appraisal after the lecture was that the topic was not suitable for young dentists. Stress, a subject on which I have written a book, many articles and lectured around the country to dentists, was not considered by young dentists to be a subject about which they should concern themselves. It is a subject which struck a chord with the audiences of older dentists to which we lectured. Stress is when the body is inappropriately in defence mode. The 'fight or flight' biochemistry and mindset are very damaging and unpleasant in such circumstanced. The inspiration for promoting awareness of and techniques for dealing with stress was from personal experience. By the age of 25 I owned two dental practices employing three associates and was planning to start up others. I was full of enthusiasm and enjoying dentistry. I could not wait to get up in the morning to go to work. I started my practicing life in a caring, helpful environment; a practice where five of us dentists gave mutual support. My move to start up my own practice was, in hindsight, premature and partly responsible for the illness which was to follow.

At twenty three I moved to England to an area populated by a large group of dentists/friends. I married, that year. The purchase of my new practice required my wife and me to move away from everyone we knew. Surprisingly it was a very lonely experience sitting in our new home with a pile of boxes. We had very little furniture as we had moved from furnished accommodation. The building up of a new practice is all consuming. Enthusiasm drives one on so that work becomes life, which although enjoyable, may lead to tiredness and stress. One does not see an emotional crisis coming. It creeps slowly but by the time there are manifestations it is deep seated.

Stress and its damaging biochemistry results from the body's response to a judgement of a situation. The origin of that judgement is experience. First experiences in any situation set a benchmark against which we compare, judge and respond to similar situations. In most cases the irrational responses will be provoked by perceived threats. For me the original irrational response was a reaction to an unfounded adverse criticism of my work. The criticism did not directly involve the patient involved, who attended me for many years afterwards. It took many months to resolve the situation and be exonerated but the incident precipitated a reaction which took years of turmoil before resolution.

It is hard to identify why the episode caused such anxiety but having been a successful conscientious student - gaining 100% quality score on all conservative work carried out over an entire year - the criticism hurt deeply. From being a dedicated practitioner I became an obsessive perfectionist. This is not said in self aggrandisement. It can only be regarded as an illness. This was not a sudden change but a slow process of continually re-examining both the process of my work and the outcomes. One area of this complex affliction was cross-infection control. In my student day it was very lax. In general practice in my earliest days it scarcely existed. Measured by today's standards, it did not exist at all. As my obsession grew we evolved systems which were perhaps even more extreme than current regulatory requirements. Even the slightest breach of the self imposed regulation caused such anxiety and worry that ever more intense adherence became essential. Coupled with this worry came guilt. Perfectionism means never being happy with the outcome. Often a patient would leave the surgery delighted with the result of my work but I would go home feeling a deep guilt knowing that I could have done it better. Gradually the condition grew into an Obsessive Compulsive Disorder which manifested itself into agoraphobia and a deep sense of guilt. This dreadful condition was underpinned by an inner strength which drove me, perhaps forced me, to continue to work during the entire illness. Each day started with the intense stress of dragging myself to work and complying with the self imposed rules and rituals. Every aspect of life was eventually involved in the constant strive to not have anything to worry about at the end of each day.

A condition such as this affects everyone about you. I still marvel that staff would work in such demanding and stressful surroundings. I owe so much to them. Not only did staff comply with my demands but I have been blessed in my practicing life by having a few extremely loyal staff. It must have been obvious that I was suffering. Whenever a member of staff left they almost invariably gave more than enough notice so that the she could train her successor in my exacting standards. My thirty seven years have been served almost entirely by six girls, each of whom left for a while and returned. These girls found the job for which they left was not as rewarding. I never discussed the condition with anyone. I know that they understood. My friends jokingly remarked on my cleanliness. I have often observed how the staff of colleagues matched their own personality. This applied to me also. I believe that I am a good judge of character. The members of staff who worked so loyally for me have similar traits to myself being in that they are thorough and dedicated but not obsessively so.

One evening I had a severe crisis; the very lowest point. I resolved then to seek help. It is difficult to describe adequately – and probably not necessary – the suffering. My home and my wife were my refuge. How she understood is difficult for me to understand. It was as if she was in constant touch with the private psychiatrist who helped me through the illness. She was not. At least I think he helped me through. I took massive doses of medication; the physical withdrawal effects from which took years to subside. Week on week I felt no improvement in the early stages. I could not see that there was another way to live. I felt that my view of the world was right and could not see how I could exist otherwise. Gradually the pressures of living in a prison of self imposed limitations essential for existence began to ease. After months of therapy when I reported that I felt so much better but then described how I still felt, my therapist remarked, **'my God where have you been?'**

At the outset he cautioned that if I went through analysis I would emerged changed. He explained that I may discover hidden abilities or that my values would change; requiring changes in lifestyle. I do not know whether I changed or just discovered my real self but my life changed. It has brought exciting opportunities. Perhaps it was that latent ability, suppressed by lack of self confidence, found expression. But that may sound conceited. There is a condition known as Creative Illness. Creative minds in all areas, science, mathematics, humour and music, through poetry, writing and art have suffered from psychosis. Perhaps it was this to which my therapist referred. 'Unless a man be born again' is the most apt phrase. When I now reflect on my earlier life it is as if I am thinking of another existence. Perhaps that is from a form of retrograde amnesia brought about by the high doses of medication which I took daily to enable me to function. The me of back then had all the drive and ambition of the 'new' - the strength which helped me through the illness - but lacked self worth. For example although I was a successful student I felt that somehow those who judged me as such did not see the real me. I felt guilty; somehow I was a fraud. The same emotion applied to every opportunity given to me in my life.

My illness was a self imposed prison, with nightmares where I had to walk through life on a single red line whilst everyone else could wander at will. This world was not policed by anyone. I just had to do it. This nightmare continued into the waking hours. The red line was policed by the fear of worry, of guilt, of harming others and of course, dirt. There was not fear of harming myself. Contamination was the means amongst a myriad of other ways by which I might harm others, not only but especially my patients. I always said that if I had a broken leg or some other tangible illness which curtailed my work, everyone would understand. But there was a stigma about my condition which meant that until now I could not talk of it.

The exhaustion of coping with the condition stemmed, I believe now, from the need to live permanently in conscious mode. We live most of our lives by subconscious programmes. Brushing ones teeth is a good example. As we brush, each morning, the subconscious runs a programme – a habit – while we get on with planning our day. Dentist spend their days telling patients with unhealthy mouths that they need to re-programme their habit by taking conscious control of their tooth brushing for a period of time so that they can change to the correct habit/technique of tooth brushing. Much of our daily activity is carried out by such habits. Many if not all readers will have had episodes of doubting that they had locked the front door or perhaps wondered having driven away from traffic lights, whether the light s had actually changed to green. This can be easily counteracted by being conscious of the act and making a conscious association with the event. **'When I closed the door, I felt the keys in my hand'.**

But imagine a life where you could not allow yourself to do anything by habit. To eradicate worry, conscious control had to be activated at all times. As the cure comes slowly and sub consciousness is once again allowed to function, one performs with far greater acuteness. The subconscious is better trained. For example one will be a better driver because of the increased awareness of everything in the immediate environment of the car and the potential threats. Emerging from the prison of OCD brings an increasing feeling of freedom. The traits do not go. That is ones personality. The extreme pressures of conscious perfectionism make way for conscientiousness and thoroughness; perhaps excellence – that is for others to judge – but the process of having analysed every action is now a benefit. A Creative Illness. My therapist was right. As I emerged from those dark unpleasant days I entered a period of intense productivity and creativity. Opportunities were offered to me for writing, TV work and public speaking. I undertook many leadership roles and from that experience wrote a book. Many business opportunities happened also. I worked twenty hours a day and enjoyed every minute of it. Perhaps this is still an obsessive personality but in an enjoyable expression. Running a marathon and other similar athletic challenges were, and still are, pursued. What has been interesting is that many of the different areas which I found to express myself could involve dentistry. I have worked for most of my practicing life in the insular world of a single handed practitioner. The early five years or so when I had associates were valuable for professional support and sustained me financially through the worst of my illness. As other areas of interest came my way, life became more enjoyable and although they required time away from the surgery I became more productive in dentistry. All of the new experiences enriched my practicing life and set new benchmarks against which I could make judgements.

It was not dentistry that caused the stress. The interplay of experience on personality had formed a basis for judgement of one's position in relationship to others. There comes a time when one succumbs to that role or has the strength to confront it. That confrontation requires the abandoning of the subconscious basis of judgement while accepting a new set of experiences as being valid.

The emotional conflict which precipitates the breakdown is multifaceted and protracted and very painful. It can be likened to a developing dispute with someone. Corrosive comments are tolerated up to a point, then, suddenly an apparently minor comment causes deep upset. Dentistry was my life in those early days. It was my means of expression of my self worth. Of course there were stressors. Such is life. So it seems obvious that the tipping point would be there. But abandoning dentistry would have gained nothing for me. The problems were within. They travelled with me and would have imprisoned me in whatever I chose to do or wherever I chose to go. Confrontation is the only solution.

## Joe Sullivan BDS, DGDP (UK) - http://jtsullivan.co.uk/

The author of **The Will to Change - From stress to success** (ISBN 1-898823-25-1). Joe Sullivan has been a GDP in a single-handed practice for 37 years. Chairman of the Dental Practitioners association from 2001 to 2008. Since 1992 he has represented GDPs in every relevant National forum and has presented seminars to dentists around England on business development, team building, self improvement and stress management.'

# Paul Tipton —"Knowledge is Power"

Solomon Ortiz once said **"Education is the key to success in life, and teachers make a lasting impact in the lives of their students"**. I am a true believer of this. No matter what age you are, education can be instrumental in your career.

As an experienced practitioner, Specialist in Prosthodontics and lecturer in cosmetic, restorative and implant dentistry, I have borne witness to the value of good post graduate education. My experience over many years has reinforced the adage 'Knowledge is Power' and I feel it is more important now than ever to invest in training, and your future.

My dentistry career started in 1978 when I qualified from Sheffield University. As a teenager a career in dentistry had not crossed my mind. I was a promising cricketer, playing for England U-19s in a test series against India and had a career as a county cricketer for Lancashire on the county staff for 5 years as an opening batsman and off-spin bowler.

As a young dentist, I was eager to learn and to build a career for myself. I knew I did not know much. At first I combined my dental career with semi-professional cricket for Cheshire for 5 years until a back injury forced me to concentrate on dentistry. A few great dentists played a crucial role in the early stages of my career. I undertook my postgraduate training with Mike Wise, Derek Setchell and Richard Ibbotson, whom I admire and respect for the encouragement they gave me to further my career and pursue my goals. The passion and enthusiasm that a great mentor can instil in you is invaluable. Everyone must have a mentor and I have been that mentor to many young dentists.

When I first started teaching in 1990, I was young and all the dentists I was training were older than me. Now the average age has come right down to under thirty years of age. Some are straight out of university, some are VTs, but most are three years post-VT, have been working in the NHS and decided they don't want to be doing "patch-up" dentistry for the next twenty to thirty years.

Over the last twenty years I have been proud to see many students of mine go on to become practice owners and lecturers in their own right. Many of today's best known dentists have been through my courses, so it's great when I see them writing articles, gaining awards and appearing on TV. One delegate has even gone on to become the Chair in Fixed Prosthodontics at the University of Southern California. The one thing that they all share is an eagerness to learn new skills and apply them practically with a little bit of help from the Tipton Education experience.

The concept of 'lifelong-learning' is more important now than ever as we face times of recession and intense competition. To remain competitive and secure even in the most difficult of times requires more than just experience, it requires skill and considerable focus.


## Surviving an Economic Downturn

For the last few years individuals and companies have had it tough and dentistry is no exception. These are challenging times for dentists, who have had or are experiencing a shortfall of private patients and income. I am convinced that there are opportunities to succeed and prosper but I think you have to be smart and you have to be knowledgeable. Education is key to surviving the economic downturn and identifying opportunities.

In difficult times smart businesses re-invent themselves to increase the gap between themselves and the competition. I believe the same holds true for dentists today. It is important that as the fees available for NHS dental work get stretched further and intervention is less well rewarded in the coming years, dentists invest in skills-building to seek out new revenue streams and remain competitive. Find an area of dentistry that you are good at and aim to be the best. Get specialist training and further qualifications from the Academies, Royal Colleges or Universities.

You must also know your limitations and refer to others. For example, don't ask me to do endo work. Nor have I ever placed an implant in my life, although I teach an Implant course – I do the restorative part of the treatment and bring in other expertise to cover the actual surgical side of implantology. I will not go beyond my own specialist area.

## Converting to Private Practice

To be competitive and successful in Private Practice, I would advise all young dentists to commit to being a continual student to gain skills but also as important, to gain confidence in their own dentistry. I would have to say that I feel some of the training young dentists now receive is not reflective of the demands of private practice. Young dentists today need to spend as much time as possible developing the skills required for private practice by investing in private education courses before making mistakes and jumping into private practice. Ask many young dentists qualifying at the moment and most want to go into private practice, some immediately with no post-graduate training!

Important areas such as Occlusion are often undervalued and yet occlusion can make cases succeed or fail. You need to understand occlusion to reduce failures in your work. Occlusion is the biggest obstacle that dentists in this country face to becoming an excellent dentist and succeeding in private practice. My advice to dentists considering the conversion to private practice is to get out there and be more proactive. Take your chances in Private Practice. It is relatively easy to grow your private business side by side with your NHS, as long as you have the skill, knowledge and confidence. Perform more private work on your NHS patients and grow that side so you're not too dependent on one mix or the other. Look at and amend all your prices, understand your price points, know and react to all your KPIs and motor onwards.

## Practice Management

I have several dentists that I work with on the business side of dentistry on a practice consultancy basis. I help dentists who have been through my courses to maximise their practice profits by teaching them business skills. This is becoming more popular in these challenging economic times.

When I'm teaching I try to ensure I cover all aspects of dental practice including marketing, selling and practice management. There's no point being the best dentist in the world if you don't have anyone coming to see you. Whether you like it or not as a dentist in general practice you are in sales and marketing. A skill also lacking in many dentists is the basic skill of running a small business. Many dentists I teach have never heard of KPI's and have no idea how to set fees, and what they're spending in relation to gross profits.

Part of my remit in training is for all dentists to have knowledge as well as communication skills. I've got no problem selling, as long as the selling is ethical. I know some dentists don't like the word 'selling', but I believe you must be able to look a patient in the eyes and be comfortable to 'sell'. We're very happy to train people to do that as it's a communication skill you can learn.

## Lab Communication

I'm an alumnus of the UCL Eastman Dental Institute and completed an MSc Degree in Conservative Dentistry in 1989. During that two-year course we had to make our own lab work so I ended up doing about thirty to forty units of lab work to fit on my own patients. I've always said that was some of the best education I ever had because it allowed me to understand the lab technician's role completely. Sadly, undergraduate dental training at the moment has very little input into what the dental technician does, and yet we are so beholden to them as dentists. There are some brilliant aesthetic dentists, such as Nitzan Bichacho, who is head of the Goldstein Aesthetics Centre at Tel-Aviv University in Israel. He will give a lecture and hold his hand up right at the beginning and say **"I'm not** great at prepping teeth but because I employ the best technician's, he now makes my restorations look fantastic, and at the end of the day the patient gets a wonderful smile".

So a technician can make you're work look fantastic and he can drag your work down in the gutter. Unless you know what the technician does and unless you work in a partnership with your technician then it is hit and miss as to whether you're going to get any better at what you do. Technician's need to be trained by dentists and vice versa. Part of my remit is to always teach dentists the technical side of Restorative and Implant Dentistry as well as the clinical and marketing side.

Dentists who have gained the relevant skills will be in a great position to capture the market. If you take your time and adhere to the correct principals, you can overcome any hurdles or pitfalls facing you in the pursuit of excellence in private dentistry. You will also be in a better position to get that "plum" job.

## Dr Paul Tipton BDS, MSc, DGDP(UK)

An internationally acclaimed Prosthodontist who has worked in private practice for more than 30 years. He lectures for Tipton Training Ltd, one of the UK's leading private dental training academies and is the author of over one 100 scientific articles for the dental press. He was voted in the Top 12 'most influential dentists in the UK' by his peers in Dentistry Magazine in April 2011.

To find out more about his well received postgraduate training courses, go to **http://www.tiptontraining.co.uk**

# Monik Vasant - General Practice for the Beginner

Having only graduated several years ago, naturally I was flattered when I was asked to write this chapter in this book. I undertook the task with some trepidation as I was conscious of the calibre of the other contributors. Nonetheless, I felt that it was appropriate to make this contribution to narrate my own experience whilst "**standing on the shoulders of giants**" so to speak.

Graduating from dental school is deservedly a joyous occasion and milestone in one's life. The impression that "you know it all" soon vanishes when you are thrown in the deep end of a general practice with no one looking over your shoulder that one is so used to in an undergraduate setting. The impression that a new graduate (by the virtue of the fact that he/she has just passed the examination) is very up-to-date could not be further from the truth as one soon realizes that *knowledge* and *application of knowledge* are two different things. Besides the text book knowledge one has acquired there is a whole new world out there. If you were given an impression at the dental school that general practice constitutes the money grabbing and ignorant sharks of the profession and that Premier League of dentists are the university academics or hospital practitioners, you may begin to question that. It is fair to say that there is a place for both. Some wish to "talk the talk" whilst others wish to "walk the walk". There will be a few who do both and balance their career as such. I have been inspired to do the latter by my mentors.

With due respect to my academic and hospital based colleagues, there is a consensus amongst various professional circles that the undergraduate course does not or cannot prepare the newly qualified for life as a GDP nor a hospital dentist. Of the four domains (Clinical, Communication Professionalism, Management and Leadership) the one which a new graduate will find most difficult are usually Communication and Management particularly the financial side of it (e.g. quoting and collecting fees from patients). One is expected to acquire these skills during the first years in practice and through postgraduate education.

The vocational trainee year is well structured and can fill many gaps but it is only the beginning and by no means an end in itself. Then taking on associateship is a giant leap forward when effectively one is running their own mini businesses. Naturally, some fail and change courses (return to a career outside of general practice or even outside of dentistry. Others thrive!).

This brings me on to my first tip. Through my work in postgraduate education I come across countless young dentists. Often they tell me their career plan after VT is to go back to dental hospital to do post graduate training/oral surgery job. I obviously think that this is important but in my opinion more important than the training itself, is its TIMING. I think it can be counterproductive to accumulate more knowledge without condensing and perfecting your existing knowledge. Often when people eventually go back into practice they are disadvantaged as they have more knowledge but even less experience to put it into practice and the lessons learnt in VT are long forgotten.

I do not blame people from thinking this is the right thing to do as just getting into Dental School is so competitive and academically focused that it seems a logical progression unless the merits of delaying further training are explained. The benefits can be countless. One can put into practice the dental school knowledge and techniques. You can assess and appraise your work over time to see how it performs e.g. It takes 5 years to assess the success of a root canal treatment. How can we see if we are any good if we don't see the patient again after a year? One can also work on developing relationships with patients and other colleagues in practice. This enables us to refine our communication skills and most importantly improves confidence in our abilities. If you appear confident to a patient and communicate effectively, you will have much more treatment acceptance and less complaints. This is an area that is overlooked by many in our profession. I have learnt so much from listening to people like Kevin Lewis on this topic and much more emphasis should be given to it.

It is important to realise that most patients do not have the foggiest idea about what extra letters we have after our names. It is how we treat them and their experience of us that holds the most weight.

How long you should stay in practice depends on where you see your future. Writing a career plan and a professional development portfolio is important in identifying your training needs. If you see yourself as a GDP or practice based specialist eventually it is definitely worth spending your early years there. There are options to do a second VT year which I think can be beneficial, provided you are still in General practice part time. If combined with an oral surgery post it can improve surgical techniques and this improves confidence whilst keeping your career options open and your hand in General practice. The MJDF qualification is general practice focused and can really improve you as a GDP.

The benefit of staying in practice depends on the practice you are in, and none are ideal for everyone. I remember being told to look for a large practice as I would learn more by working with more practitioners. There is some merit in this, but I would not look at it in isolation. You could work in a fantastic two surgery practice with a knowledgeable mentoring Principal and conversely you could be in a huge practice where everyone is doing their own thing and the Principal is too busy to help. The important factors are the structure of the practice and the personality of the Principal. Ask yourself;

- **Does he/she seem understanding?**
- **Have they kept up to date with their professional education?**
- **Are they doing the sort of dentistry you would like to do?**
- **Does the practice seem friendly?**
- **Is the equipment good?**
- **Can you see yourself working for a few years in your potential surgery?**

I am sure you get the gist but the most important thing above else is **DO NOT MAKE A DECISION BASED ON FINANCIAL REASONS ALONE** at this stage, as it often only gives a short term gain. An NHS practice offering a lower UDA rate where everything feels right is often better than a higher UDA rate practice that feels wrong. If the practice fits your criteria, you will feel good and perform better. Within time the financial difference will be gone and you will be in a stronger position for your future. This especially applies when agreeing to numbers of contracted UDA's. Agreeing to more than you are capable of **comfortably** may seem financially attractive, but if you are over stretched you will make compromises with either your work or your patient relationships, both of which will negatively affect your finances. Early in your career, your techniques should be getting **refined** not **ruined**. Again a short term gain will end up with a long term loss, as when the NHS system changes (soon) or you want to work privately you will have problems. The more you work in the ideal way the quicker and better you will get, so don't worry about earning less and taking time with treatments in the beginning.

After a few years as a GDP you may get itchy feet to do some postgraduate training. I worked for four years as a GDP and then decided to do a one day a month course. I found it very rewarding and I would advocate initially doing your postgraduate education like this if you want to be a GDP long term. The benefits are that you constantly get to practice any new knowledge, there is less of a financial impact as you earnings are protected and if you come across something that wets your appetite you can then always go and do a formal masters or further specialist training. You generally do not get any extra letters after your name for doing private courses but they can be invaluable. I would initially choose a course that gives you a sound knowledge of restorative dentistry and occlusion as it underpins most of our work. Young dentists often immediately go for courses on the "sexy" subjects like implants and cosmetic dentistry. These specialties are hard and you need a good restorative base beyond dental school knowledge to be successful. Ignoring this can be a recipe for disaster. Some courses offer clinical mentoring following completion which really helps. I found that doing a series of year long private post graduate courses focused me to the sort of work I wanted to do and after seven years in practice I decided to do a Masters degree.

Another aspect I would like to touch upon is becoming a Principal as most young dentists I speak to say they would like to be one. My earlier points are much more valid if this is the case. You should definitely ensure you are comfortable in your own abilities and experienced in general practice before taking on this hugely difficult task.

Setting up in practice is daunting and can be an inordinate amount of work and risk, for sometimes not much gain. Some principals actually earn less than their associates due to the increasing costs of running a business, therefore careful planning, execution and management is needed to be successful. Your personality dictates whether you would enjoy it and if you do it prepare for potentially amazing days and some unbelievably awful ones.

A common question is that is it better to set up a new (aka squat) practice or buy an existing one. There are pros and cons to each but it can be easier to take over a practice which is already running and profitable. Any changes can be done at your own pace. The down side to this can be that you pay a premium for them and taking over the existing staff and ensuring the practice complies with new legislation can be difficult.

Setting up a squat practice is no easy feat and can still be costly. Brand new equipment, just like cars, drops in value the second you buy it. Professional services like architects, designers and legal fees are all costly and have no future value but in most cases are needed. You start with no income and no patients so a lot more work is required and a lot more can go wrong. Starting a new NHS practice gives guaranteed income but contracts are now few and far between, so for many looking to do this private practice may be only way. The BDA have some great advice sheets on setting up in practice and I would strongly suggest becoming a member to get access to all this information. However I would like to list some key tips from lessons that I learnt from setting up a squat practice.

Research the type of practice you want. Then highlight an area and strategy and put together a meticulous business plan for the banks or anyone else looking to invest in you. In the current climate getting finance is hard so organise this first. Information on writing a business plan is available on the internet. If you find that funding is limited then look at leasing a premises, rather than buying. This means you need less money initially but you are renting someone else's building so you will have a landlord.

Having an experienced partner who already has a practice can help provided that you have the same vision and goals. This can help funding as the experienced partner can have more of a silent role but supply funds and advice while you do the daily running. Obviously you must trust each other. Your roles must be clear from the outset and you need a partnership agreement that clearly states your responsibilities, splitting of profits/losses and what happens should you want to end the partnership (as it will end eventually). If the percentage split reflects your contribution accurately then this can be a very good way to get yourself on the practice ladder.

A building needs to have D1 planning permission to use it as a dental practice. Premises with this tend to be sparse but look out for old health clinics as these will have it. Identifying a premises which has D1 is ideal as it saves time. If not you need to apply to change the buildings use, therefore you will need an architect to design your surgery and draw plans. This can be expensive. Do not purchase a property or sign a lease until you have confirmed you have D1 planning. It can take several months to get D1 planning and a seller or landlord can generally pullout at any time. A solicitor may be able to tie sellers/landlords into an agreement subject to planning permission being granted. There is so much risk here so it is important you get expert advice from architects before you start, about the likelihood of a building getting planning permission. Residential areas are harder to get planning permission for, as local residents can object. A common reason for planning permission refusal can come from the highways department as they prefer practices to have their own car parks. Their ideal is three off road parking spaces per surgery and a car park needs to have a turning circle. This is not as critical if you are in a town centre or there is a public car park nearby. Be careful with property where significant building work is required or where there is no room for future expansion.

Agree a fixed fee with architects to draw plans and get planning permission. Most prefer to work on a time basis and their fees can really rack up. Get a few quotes from reputable firms ideally ones with a close relationship with the local planning department. Get dental design experts to help your architect draw up the plans and ensure your design allows for future expansion i.e. more surgeries. If you feel you may want to extend the building it can be useful to get permission for this at the same time.

Once you have planning permission get your architect to do a specification. This is like a shopping and instruction list for your project. This enables you to put your project out to tender to builders which saves you money, whilst ensuring that all people are quoting like for like. It also reduces the risk of being invoiced by builders for unplanned extras. Ideally use a reputable builder (good luck) that your architect has experience with and avoid suspiciously low quotes. It is often better to pay slightly more and have peace of mind.

Ensure you have someone managing the whole project to ensure the various contractors on the project work together efficiently i.e. the electrician completes his work before the plasterer begins his and the dental equipment company have all the correct services put in place prior to installation. This sounds obvious but it is crucially important and failure to have someone "pulling the strings" can result in more expense or a compromised result. Remember however good the individual contractors are, their main concern is their personal task. If you draw parallels with an orchestra even the best individual musicians need an experienced conductor.

Get advice from your accountant as to the most tax efficient way to structure your new business and purchase equipment. Get quotes from different equipment suppliers and when deciding make sure to consider the length of warranty, maintenance program, proximity and cost of local engineers should you have a problem. Do not be over ambitious with the amount of surgeries you equip and delay non essential expensive equipment until you really need it. There is no point in spending money or running down warranty on idle equipment. It is definitely worth designing and putting in the services i.e. plumbing and wiring, for future surgeries, but just equip the surgeries that will be working initially and you can buy as you grow.

Set a marketing budget to help drive patients into your practice. Web marketing can work well. Using a specialist dental company costs more but it means less work for you. If they are good it will be worth every penny.

Your key staff must have experience i.e. head nurse, but having others with none and training them to your desired standard can be a good way to get the staff you want and minimise your initial expenditure. You also inherit less bad habits from other practices. Several companies exist that source and train nurses for you in house for a reasonable cost.

Once established take time out to work on the practice rather than in it. People working four days clinically often earn the same as full timers. Always try to think like a patient rather than a dentist.

Managing staff is one of the hardest challenges. Some companies, for a reasonable fee, will look after all your employment law compliance i.e. contracts, dispute management, health and safety at work. This expertise can be invaluable and the added benefit is that they cover the cost of any staff related legal issues provided you have followed their advice.

When leading you team pick your battles wisely. Ensure the things that can ruin your business are prevented from happening rather than worrying about very small issues that will not really impact. The danger of constantly getting on people's backs is that they will stop listening.

Networking with local businesses, colleagues and at social events can be a very good way of growing your business profile. Always carry business cards as you never know who you might bump into.

These tips are just my opinions based on what I had to go through and are not exhaustive. Some people may feel differently about certain aspects and that is to be expected.

One last tip I would give is that I am no genius and most of what I have learnt has come from listening to successful people. The UK has some of the most talented and knowledgeable people in the dental world, many of whom have contributed to this book. Organisations like the BDA and Dental Protection Ltd have a wealth of useful knowledge and resources available to members of all ages. I would strongly recommend any young dentist to identify people who you respect and find out what they have to say and how they got to where they are. You don't have to re-invent the wheel.

# Dr Monik Vasant BChD

# Ian Wilson – Stuck

Going up to the 9th floor with all 4 kids for a Saturday afternoon treat seemed like a good idea as we bundled ourselves into the brand new lift! I lived in Mwanza, Tanzania from 2002 till 2011, where a new shiny lift is a breakthrough in entertainment. It was all going to plan until someone from the national grid decided to put the kettle on and everything went very black and stationary half way between the 6th and 7th floors! Jake grabs one arm, Imani grabs a leg, Neema grabs my throat...tightly and Maisha just screamed. Body contorted and slowing going blue i ask myself what should I do?

a.   **Scream with the kids?...no!**

b.   **Throw the kids into the black void of the lift and bang hysterically on the door?...no!**

c.   **Stay calm and reassure the kids that this is OK, the lights will come back on in a minute and we can get on with our 'treat'...even when inside I'm feeling that a] and b] seem a lot more helpful for self preservation....Oh yes!**

60 seconds later after what seemed 60 minutes, the lights came on, I was a hero because  I had said they would and we got on with our treat with free drinks from the hotel for being so brave!

At that time there were several lessons to learn...when next for you, your family or your organisation...*the lights go out and everything grinds to a halt*...remember a few things.

1.   **It hasn't...the potential is there for the lights to come on and things to get moving again.**

2.   **People around you will get scared and look to you for leadership whether you feel like it or not.**

3.   **It's ok to scream...just do it on the inside or with people outside the immediate situation.**

4.  **Don't lose sight of the dreams of where you want to be….you will get the chance to achieve them again**

5.  **Don't ever get into a lift with 4 young children in a multi storey building in Mwanza, Tanzania**

Looking back to when I first qualified I remember how quickly the day to day routine of work, finance, family and just life slowly chipped away at all my aspirations. They were still there but somehow after a few years of dental practice, there was that sense of being 'stuck' and I needed to lift my horizons again to get my perspective back on my dental career…it was time to take a risk!

**Risky Business?...get a life**

Every year groups of 22 volunteers have gone to Tanzania to take a risk and be part of our Dental Volunteer training programme with **Bridge2Aid**. Whether they are there for the first time or returners, they are all willing to step out of their daily business and take a risk, but for what? Coming from the relative comfort of the UK they are people who have realised that in whatever walk of life, 'It's easier to make a profit…..it's a lot tougher to make a difference!'

Wanting to make a difference costs in time, energy, resources but for all of our volunteers they want to make a difference not only for themselves but for others.

Churchill said, **"We make a living by what we get, but we make a life by what we give."**

Lifting my own horizons in the early nineties and seeing how my 'risky business' could only give someone in a developing nation a life but also I would discover another dimension to my own! What followed was a decade of volunteering into areas of East & West Africa to take my growing skills and experience in clinical Dentistry to bring pain relief and oral health services to vast communities who had no access to the simplest extraction.

Taking the risky step to move out to Tanzania as a family in 2002 and see Bridge2Aid grow as friends and colleagues joined us and brought their unique contribution was a risk…but a risk worth taking.

However, could it be that other people 'get a life'?....you would need to ask our volunteers about that, but what can be said is this, "Only those who will risk going too far can possibly find out how far one can go! I would urge you that if you could take one lifetimes opportunity to serve the poor in the developing world you will not only dramatically change another's life...you might up changing your own. All our volunteers comment on how the experience changes their attitudes [for the better!] towards all the aspects of their clinical practice in the UK.

''We never will discover new lands and horizons without consenting to leave the shore behind''

### Risky business?...get a life!

Don't kick it...fix it! 120kph in BMW or Merc is a pleasant experience but in a Suzuki Vitara! On that day a driver was taking me from the foothills of Kilimanjaro to the airport he thought it must be on my list of 50 things to do before I die...and he also assumed it was now in the No 1 spot! It gets better!...I had spotted him and his buddy 'kicking' the rear tyre [this being the globally recognised technique by men who know nothing about cars!] as we were about to leave and so as our speed reached Mach 3 we were soon greeted by the same rear tyre expiring dramatically. What follows is Monty Python-esque...both guys getting out and.... 'kicking' the tyre again!..as if that was going to inflate it into action! The problem with all of this....it was Andie's birthday and I NEEDED TO GET BACK or I was dead and in my Suzuki speed machine there was no jack, no wheel brace but a trendy spare wheel cover!

Thankfully after heated phone calls and a journey to Arusha airport breaking all known land speed records we got there in time, Andie had a fab birthday and I was the most wonderful man ever...well at least for one day!

So what's my point? Sometimes even after all these years I can get involved in a project, scheme...whatever without really thinking it through! Zeal and enthusiasm flood through my being and wash all out all know reason and strategic thinking...invariably it ends in tears and me kicking it not fixing it! So much pain and grief could have been avoided had I sat down with other trusted friends and colleagues and simply asked for help to plan.

So the next time you set out on a journey or a project or an initiative, please, please make sure that you have the tools you need for plans A, B and Z. Also if you suspect there are issues before your start then don't just kick it...please fix it first...120 kph is a lot more pleasant after that.

### Please fly the plane

'It's a little bumpy' said the pilot as we got in the plane to travel to the next clinic...the plane being a 6 seater light aircraft and the clinic being at a remote Gold mine somewhere near the Kenyan border. 20 minutes later Mary our Tanzanian nurse is decidedly 'green' which means she is not well as normally she is definitely black! For many years in Tanzania my 'commute' was a light aircraft from Mwanza where we lived as Bridge2Aid team and families out to rural Gold mines where as part of the Hope Dental Centre operations we had the fun and privilege of setting up dental clinics for employees and local community.

As we climb I then notice that the pilot is not flying the plane and in fact his No2 is! I realise that this is often done to get trainees experience...HOWEVER...as Mary is now considering a skydiving career from our current 12,000ft...I had to do what most people don't like...CONFRONT. 'Excuse me' tapping the pilot..."**Will YOU please fly the plane!"**

Confrontation always brings a response...it took less than 20 seconds for the pilot to take the controls back and persuade Mary to unstrap her parachute and close the door! Later when we were back on the ground I explained fully to the pilot...passengers want to see the pilot flying the plane and when they don't see that they get jumpy and lose confidence. Next time they won't want to fly with you and will go to somebody else! He got the message.

Quick question – What is it that we do or say that makes people lose confidence in us? In our daily working situations, are there 'messages' that we are sending out to our teams, colleagues & friends that instead of bringing confidence are resulting in the exact opposite? Our colleagues and families want us to show the way…to take the lead…to 'Fly the Plane'…not someone or something else! Don't wait till someone taps you on the shoulder and confronts you which can be painful. Change before you have to! Why not go to a trusted team member and ask if there are 'things that could do with changing that will bring confidence to all that you do…and maybe stop a colleague or family member putting on their parachute!

## At the next roundabout take the 2nd exit

Coming back recently in the car from visiting cousins over the weekend, I thought the sat-nav was having a moment of overload! For each instruction from 'the lady of the little black box' came another female voice immediately repeating the exact same line…word for word and far more charming! I slapped the little black box a couple of times to help sat-nav lady 'get a grip' but the repeating kept on coming…and her voice was getting cuter! Our little 3 yr old Maisha sitting behind us is being entered for 'cute child sat-nav voice 2011' because she had sat-nav lady down word for word, expression for expression, tone for tone! What she heard, she became! Simple!

For those of us who lead people let us be aware of the quote, **"If you hear how wonderful you are often enough, you begin to believe it, no matter how you try to resist it."** I am often aware of leaders who forget to thank and praise their team on a regular basis and then get upset when objectives don't get achieved, people aren't engaged or the team seems fractured. Sadly I am also aware of leaders who are continually critical of their teams and then wonder why stuff doesn't get done!

We have such an opportunity to create 'family' in our dental teams but unless we enthuse, encourage, mentor, bring discipline & direction, bestow value and appreciation then the family will be pretty dysfunctional. You might say 'I can't do that stuff!!'…OK then get someone in to help you. I can't recommend Chris Barrow any higher as a friend and colleague who will 'coach' you and your team into becoming the productive 'family' you want your practice team to be. If you want to get in touch with Chris then visit him on…

If you want your team to be confident, self assured, great communicators, innovative, owners of the vision and motivated, in fact all the things you want them to be, then let them hear it plenty of times from you!

**What your team will hear, they will become. Simple!**

What was 'small & scary!'…after 8 yrs…it is finally the beginning During 2003, I had the opportunity to meet with Dr Rob Barbour the medical director for Barrick Gold. Together we discussed the needs for his Gold mine employees and their immediate families to access oral health services.

Within a week I was in a VERY small plane, with a small mobile dental kit, portable chair and a pilot who just wondered where all this stuff would go and whether the plane would get airborne!…it was only a 3 seater. Small & scary! Since that time Bridge2Aid has had the privilege and excitement of pioneering in partnership with Barrick Gold and Anglo Gold; a model approach of providing access to oral health services to their various mine sites in Tanzania.

Over the last 8 years we have together established dental clinics in Bulyanhulu, Tulawaka, Buzwagi, North Mara & Geita gold mines. These clinics have been fully kitted out which enables our dental teams to provide cost effective and quality dental care to the mining workforce, keeping them pain free and providing preventative services. Not only have the clinical services been established but from these valued partnerships and with the ministry of Health, we have been able to expand the training model of Oral Urgent treatment through DVP (Dental Volunteer programme) into the rural communities surrounding the mines.

In May 2011, was my last mine visit and my last time in the light aircraft (thankfully much bigger these days). My last time providing care for appreciative mine employees. My last time working with colleagues on site. 8 years later it was finally beginning!

It may be my final visit but I am glad that it is only the beginning of the next phase of development of the mining services. There is a great Bridge2Aid team now in Tanzania and under a great leadership team there is continued scope to develop the services to bring the very best dental care to the mine & their surrounding communities.

What started so small and scary [how we fitted the kit in the plane and actually took off I'll never know] has now become a service that contributes to the dental care for thousands. I'm glad that starting 'small & scary' worked for us. It was allowed to grow naturally as the services we developed brought confidence and competence to every member of the team. 'Small and scary' allowed us to adapt where needed and to remain flexible enough to take advantage of new opportunities very quickly without the need for committee or huge resources.

Looking back to when we first started Hope Dental Centre…another example of 'small and scary' but worth it! Taking old storage rooms in a hotel in Mwanza city and being able to transform it into a 2 surgery dental centre not only was inspirational for me doing it but brought such enthusiasm from colleagues here in the UK that a momentum began of involvement and buy in to help develop and resource the project. I wonder if as you read this that there is a 'small and scary' or even a 'huge and terrifying' project waiting for you to get it going. I'm no expert on this but all I know that with vision, passion, determination, faith and great friends around you anything is possible. I hope that perhaps 8 yrs from now you will be like me saying, 'It's finally the beginning'

## Cruise Control

On the road with the family we had the joy of driving through a 3000 mile stretch of average speed cameras for road works where, yes you guessed it, there was millions of cones but no road works! Wanting to be a good citizen and not exceed the speed limit, unlike those others who passed me, [You know who you are!] I put on the cruise control in anticipation of being at the same speed for the rest of my life! Now we didn't break the speed limit, we didn't break the law, but we did break the wills of the drivers in the long queue behind us! Cruise control on a car has its benefits but in leadership and life terms it is dangerous!

- **It is boring [at one point I thought of getting out, going for a walk and I'm sure I would have rejoined the car quite safely later]**
- **It is limiting [We we're overtaken at one point by a bike!]**
- **It saps creativity makes you unproductive and can breed inactivity.**

The problem is it is also safe, secure, innocent and can be seen as cautious or prudent! There are a million reasons out there to live on cruise control and some are beyond our own control. We may find cruise control is helpful for a season but we must never live in that place as a matter of lifestyle and habit.

For us, in Bridge2Aid, we understand there is the need for caution, confidence and prudence especially when it comes to how we use the resources of our amazing donors, supporters and friends. However we must never have a cruise control mentality where we might lose our ability to innovate, take risks and be productive for the benefit of the thousands of people in pain through dental disease! If today life seems to be in cruise control...there is a switch on the bottom left hand side that says, "Off".

### For crying out loud

Last year, I had the memorable occasion of a tear gas grenade in my front garden. Not that the police were after me at all but because of where we lived we got caught up in the aftermath of election results in Tanzania. The kids ran around the house with damp cloths on their faces playing 'run from the smoke' and 'hold your breath as long as you can'...they had a blast...meanwhile Andie and I had tears streaming down our faces as we closed curtains to stop the gas and the kids thinking we're upset because they won the 'hiding from the gas' games. Moments of confusion, tears and pain with no real solution but to wait it out…

A few weeks later I had one of the most sobering moments of my life, visiting the genocide memorial museum in Kigali, Rwanda. For those hundreds of thousands of people, for 100 days; moments of confusion tears and pain with no real solution but to wait it out. There was nowhere to go, no one to defend them despite the cries for help to a watching world. No hope! In my safe and cosy world the danger is that I can be so busy '**doing what I do**' that I can easily miss the warning signs of people's tears of pain and become hard of hearing to their cries for help.

Today I discovered there are 6 dentists in a country of 11 million people, another example of people in pain, needing help but with no real solution but to be in pain and wait it out! Wherever we are and whoever we are, there are people in pain for many varied reasons who need us to be part of their solution, to act now on their behalf and to be the hope they wish for! All we have to do is understand and respond

This doesn't necessarily apply that all of us will go overseas and volunteer though! What about the people we work within our dental teams on a day to day basis. Most people would rather you as a leader heard their 'story' than grant their requests! Rather than waiting for the next 'explosion' to hit our team dynamic is it not possible to spend time hearing & understanding the journey our team members are on. No team is ever perfect but where I have seen dental practice teams spend time together outside their clinical hours and people become 'known & understood' then when the problems do '**suddenly come over the fence without warning**' there is a relational [and not just functional] team to respond and resolve the issues.

## I Believe

I believe that everyone in the **Bridge2Aid** family and in your team or Dental practice has strengths! You may wish you had some others but you have got what you have and they are great! I believe that no one has got quite the same combination as gifts as you…there is no normal…only you and it works…well!  I believe that you are the most productive, most satisfied, most happy, most fulfilled, most inspirational to those around you…when you work and play to your strengths…the things you like and are good at!

I believe that everyone wins: team, colleagues, family, everyone when you do that and play to your strengths. BUT!

It doesn't matter what I believe…it only matters what YOU believe! Let each day be that day when we all move that little but closer in placing our energy and passions into what we love to do and where we feel most fulfilled…because then and only then will we all see the best that is within you.

**Dr Ian Wilson**

**www.bridge2aid.org**